POL

MW00476294

Berlin

*With 17 illustrations
and 18 maps and charts*

GENERAL INFORMATION

EXPLORING BERLIN – ROUTES

POLYGLOTT-VERLAG
MÜNCHEN

Published by the Polyglott-Redaktion
Author: Frauke Burian
Adapted for American readers by Donald Arthur
Illustrations: Vera Solymosi-Thurzó
Maps and Charts: Eberhart von Harsdorf
Cover photo: Klaus Lehnartz

*

We would like to thank the Berlin Tourist Bureau and Marian Wajselfisz, Berlin,
for their help and support.

We are always happy to receive comments for later editions.
Please write to:
Polyglott-Verlag, Redaktion, Postfach 40 11 20, D-8000 München 40.

All information dates from October 1990.
Every care has been taken to insure accuracy,
but the publishers can accept no responsibility for errors or omissions.

*

The numbers in brackets after the names of the
various sights correspond to numbers on the map.

Colored numbers at the sides of the pages
refer to route numbers.

*

5th Edition · 1991/92
© 1987 by Polyglott-Verlag Dr. Bolte KG, München
Printed in Germany / Druckhaus Langenscheidt, Berlin / W. III. Eb
(Library of Congress Registration)
ISBN 3-493-61398-9

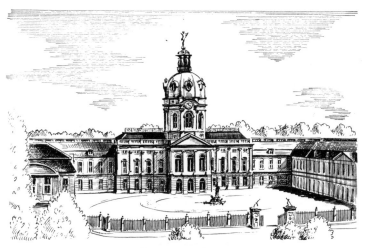

Charlottenburg Palace

Berlin

In 1987, East and West Berlin held separate celebrations of the city's 750th anniversary on both sides of what seemed at the time to be a permanent, impenetrable wall. Hardly anyone could have imagined that only two years later the East German government, which always claimed to be a "people's democracy", would be forced to capitulate to a "gentle revolution" inspired by the motto: "*We* are the people!" Today, after symbolizing the Cold War for over 28 years, that Wall, where over eighty people paid for their desire for freedom with their lives, is no more. West Berlin has ceased to be an island, and visitors to both sides of the city are now cordially welcomed to visit such previously inaccessible East German destinations as Potsdam, Rheinsberg, Neuruppin and the Spree Forest. Indeed, the German Democratic Republic itself lasted less than a year after that memorable November 9th. On October 3rd, 1990, the post-war era came to an end. Germany was reunited, and Berlin again became one city. The last remnants of the Wall are now on display in museums, as silent testimony of man's inhumanity to man.

Now that the euphoria has died down, a period of sober reflection about the future of this historical city has begun. A new controversy, even within the ranks of the major political parties, has arisen. While the unification treaty specifically stipulates that Berlin is capital of the country, for all intents and purposes the seat of government has remained in what was largely touted as the stop-gap solution of Bonn. Today, the jury is still out on this one. – Beyond this, the city faces an enormous clean-up task: housing is at a premium, and the eastern part of the city is in urgent need of major reconditioning. Moreover, just about every public issue, from postal delivery to the traffic laws, will need readjustment to accommodate the newly reunited municipality. A predictable increase in travel to the city is certain to require expansion of both Tegel Airport in the former western part of the city and Schönefeld in what was once East Berlin, and the railway facilities will also need overhauling. Subway stations in East Berlin that were walled up for decades have been reopened, but they too will need plenty of refurbishment before they are on a par with facilities in the west.

Berlin's cultural community is determined to join forces and return the city to its former status as a capital of the arts and sciences. Museum collections are being reorganized; theatres, opera houses and symphony orchestras are polishing up their already ambitious repetoires; Babelsberg Studios, where the likes of Marlene Dietrich and Billy Wilder got their start, are due for a face-lift, and plans are currently under way to promote coopera-

3

tive projects amongst the various institutions of higher learning. In short, a city which for years was primarily known internationally as a political curiosity, "the divided city", is now preparing to resume its rightful place beside London, Paris, Florence and New York as one of the cultural high points of the world.

Location and Area

Berlin is sprawled in the heart of Europe. Its easterly longitude is 13 degrees 25 minutes, the same line as Naples. Its northerly latitude of 52 degrees 31 minutes is the same as London's. The city lies between the Mittelgebirge Mountain Range and the Baltic Coast in the middle of the Mark Brandenburg on the Spree and Havel Rivers. Berlin is Germany's largest city both in area and population. Larger in area than New York City, Greater Berlin would easily accommodate the cities of Cleveland, Boston, Atlanta and San Francisco inside its borders with room to spare. Berlin's average elevation is between approximately 115 and 200 ft. above sea level. The city covers an aggregate area of 341 square miles, of which the western section comprises 185 square miles (54.4%) and the eastern 156 square miles (45.6%). The developed area in the western section accounts for a little more than a third of the city's entire area; in the eastern section somewhat less than half of the area has been developed. In the western part of Berlin 21 square miles are used agriculturally, in the eastern 36; in the western part 30 square miles are forest area, 31 in the eastern; in the western part 12 square miles are public water areas, in the eastern 9 square miles; in the western section 17 square miles are park areas, in the eastern 18.5 square miles. The district of Köpenick with its 24.6 square miles of forest is by far the frontrunner in terms of forest area. Berlin can justifiably be called "The City in the Country".

Landscape, Lakes and Rivers

Berlin, located on the edge of an ancient ice age river valley, has only very low elevations, such as the *Müggelberge* (377 ft.), the *Schäferberg* (337 ft.), the *Havelberg* (318 ft.), the 259-feet *Karlsberg,* crowned by the Grunewald Tower, and the *Kreuzberg* (217 ft.). In addition, it has a couple of artificial hills, the so-called rubble mountains, built of rubble from the ruins of the war. They include the *Teufelsberg* in Grunewald (known locally as Mount Trash), which, at 378 feet, represents the highest elevation in Berlin, the *Insulaner* (246 ft.) in Schöneberg and the *Humboldthöhe* (282 ft.) in the *Humboldthain.*

The city lies on the Spree and Havel Rivers. The *Spree,* which has its source in the Lausitz Region, flows through the *Great Müggelsee* inside the Berlin city limits, flows past both sides of the "Museum Island" in East Berlin, then flows into the *Havel* near Spandau. The Havel in turn forms the loveliest of Berlin's lakes, the *Tegeler See,* the *Stössensee* and the *Wannsee.* In all, Berlin contains no less than 62 lakes and 127 other bodies of water such as tributaries and canals (and has more bridges than Venice). No other large city in Germany has so much recreation area within its city limits as does Berlin. A few of these places are as crowded as the Kurfürstendamm on weekends. Great hordes of people go pouring out to the *Grunewaldsee* (easy to get to from the downtown area), the *Schlachtensee,* the *Krumme Lanke, Havelchaussee,* the *Wannsee* and the *Müggelsee.* In remoter areas, you may not find a soul, for instance in the *Spandau, Tegel* and *Düppel Forests,* the latter in the southern part of Berlin, where visitors can wander among the wide variety of trees (the notion that all of Berlin's woods are full of pine trees is a fable), past small marshes and swamps, tiny lakes and ponds. According to local statistics, Berliners have some 15 square miles of woods at their disposal.

Climate

Berlin is situated in a transfer zone between an oceanic and a continental climate with westerly winds predominating. The "Berliner Luft", Berlin's world-renowned bracing, dry air (the legend continues despite the occasional smog alarm) is a result of the expansive forests, which function as an air filter. Relatively dry weather is the general tone of Berlin's climate. The city's annual precipitation of 23 inches is well below the national average. The average annual temperature has been calculated at 49 degrees Fahrenheit, with the median for the lowest month (January) 34 degrees F. and the highest monthly average (July) 66 degrees F.

Population

Berlin's population has a wide variety of sources. While the city's population was initially dominated by Germans from the area of the *Lower Rhine,* it later took on a different aspect thanks to large migrations from the east: from *Silesia* and *Pomerania,* today part of Poland, and *East Prussia,* now divided between Poland and the Soviet Union. At the beginning of the 18th century around 6,000 French *Huguenots* fled their homeland for Berlin, where they were quickly assimilated – today, certain pages in the Berlin phone book give the casual observer the feeling he might be in Paris or Montreal. Like many of the world's greatest cities, Berlin has always thrived on persons from other places. But whereas over the last few decades they came mainly from the West, since the opening of the Wall the influx has been increasingly from the East, from Poland and the former East Germany.

Berlin numbers some 3,400,000 inhabitants today (as against 4,500,000 in 1943). Of these, around 2,100,000 live in the western section and a good 1,300,000 in the eastern. The actual population count is probably around 100,000 higher, owing to the fact that a large number of the foreigners living in this part of the city entered West Berlin illegally.

According to official records, there are currently 273,000 foreigners living in the western section, 120,000 of them from *Turkey*, 31,000 from *Yugoslavia*, 16,200 from *Poland*, 8,000 from *Italy* and 7,000 from *Greece*. The foreign population, mostly so-called "quest workers", lives primarily in the districts of Schöneberg, Neukölln and Kreuzberg – the last of these, the smallest and most densely populated district in the city, is known to the locals as "Little Istanbul". 28 percent of the people living here are foreign nationals, primarily Turks. The size of the foreign population in the eastern part of the city is negligible. It is estimated that in the next 20 years the population of the greater Berlin area will increase about one million.

With 1,458 residents per square mile, Berlin is the most densely populated city in Germany. The population density in the eastern section of the city is, on the average, 1,224 residents per square mile. The most heavily populated district is Prenzlauer Berg with a population density of 5,134 per square mile, the lowest Köpenick with 337 residents per square mile.

Berliners and their Language

The great German poet Johann Wolfgang von Goethe described the Berliners as an "audacious race" whom one could only outwit by giving as good as one got, if not even a little better. This statement refers to the legendary "Berliner Schnauze", or Berlin quick lip, a trait virtually unknown to other parts of the country. Berlin's wisecrackers have a smart remark for every occasion, a penchant for deflating the self-important ("Spats he's got – but no socks!") and a cynical attitude toward sacred cows looked upon with unsullied adoration by the rest of the nation.

Typical of Berlin wit are the nicknames given by the natives to many of the sacrosanct local temples of culture and government, of which the two best known are the "pregnant oyster" for the Congress Center and "Circus Karajani", the name for the New Philharmonic Hall.

Economy

Despite the division of the city and its disadvantageous location (compensated for in the case of West Berlin by subsidies from the Federal Republic of Germany), today's Berlin remains the largest industrial city in Germany. In the western part of the city more than 800,000 people are gainfully employed, around 40 % of them in the production of goods (industry, manufacturing, etc.). The largest industrial sector is the *electrical industry* (35 %), followed by the *grocery and delicatessen industry* (12.8 %) and *machine construction* (9.3 %). Industrial Berlin has left its imprint on various parts of the city now named for the mammoth corporations which operate there – "Borsig's Woods" and "Siemens City" are just two examples. The *chemical* and *clothing industries* have also taken on great significance. The *tourist trade* is the sixth largest industry in the city's economy. In the eastern part of the city the electrical industry is the largest industry, followed by the machinery, transportation, grocery and chemical industries.

Construction and Reconstruction

At the end of the Second World War, Berlin was almost completely destroyed. More than a sixth of all the ruined buildings in Germany could be found in the capital alone. Only 30 % of the city's buildings survived the war.

Residential construction in the western part began in 1949. To date, a good 500,000 new dwellings have been constructed here, about 80 % of them in publicly financed "social housing projects". Several completely new neighborhoods came into being, most of them in the outlying districts – of these *Gropius City* (named for the renowned German-American architect) in Britz-Buckow-Rudow (in the Neukölln District) and the *Märkisches Viertel* in Reinickendorf are the best known and the most frequently deplored, often cited as horrible examples of depersonalized residential architecture or, to use a Berlinism, "barracks for rent". The *Hansaviertel* (see p. 29) on the edge of the Tiergarten District enjoys a better reputation. The buildings represent a large

5

variety of housing styles in natural surroundings, even though the whole complex is only minutes away from downtown Berlin. The "Interbau '57" fair marked the start of the *Convention Hall* in the Tiergarten District, then considered the boldest piece of architecture in Europe, and of the *Corbusier Skyscraper*. Today, as in many other places, the city planners of Berlin have learned by the mistakes of the past. They have realized that housing means more than just a roof over the resident's head, and they have transferred the main thrust of their activities to the preservation and modernization of existing residential properties. The 1987 International Building Exposition (IBA) has seen the creation of some forward-looking housing complexes, e.g. in *Tiergarten* and in *Kreuzberg*, where great care has been taken to modernize many of the old buildings. Half of the IBA buildings have been completed, the rest are under construction or in the planning stage. Even so, there are still apartment barracks from the end of the last century in *Kreuzberg, Schöneberg, Neukölln* and *Wedding*, primarily inhabited by foreign workers, senior citizens and university students. Unlike in the United States, where most students live on campus, German students are almost equally divided between university residence facilities and commuting to lectures and seminars from other parts of town.

Most public and cultural buildings are also products of the last three decades: the buildings of the Free University and the Technical University, the University Clinic in Steglitz, museum buildings, the *Europa Center* shopping and recreation mall and similar, slightly less lively centers in other parts of town ("Ku'damm-Eck", "Ku'damm-Karree"). On the southern edge of the Tiergarten District, a new cultural center, to be called the *Culture Forum* on Kemperplatz, is now nearing completion. This center was begun in 1963 with the construction of the *Philharmonie Concert Hall* and expanded in 1968 with the completion of the *National Gallery*. The new building for the *State Library* (1978) has also been completed, as have the *Musical Instruments Museum* (1984) and the *Museum of Applied Arts* (1985), on either side of the Philharmonie. The *Concert Hall for Chamber Music* opened its doors in the fall of 1987.

In the eastern section of the city 334,500 new housing units were built from 1949 to 89. In *Marzahn, Hohenschönhausen* and *Hellersdorf* suburbs for several hundred thousand people were established. They were constructed with prefabricated panels in the monotonous and dreary style predominant throughout the G.D.R.

Work began on the reconstruction and/or restoration of great portions of the downtown area – Unter den Linden, Platz der Akademie, Nikolaiviertel – in 1961. Near the *Museum Island* a building for scholarship and culture was constructed, on *Marx-Engels Platz* government buildings. On the spot where the Berlin Town Palace once stood, the massive showpiece *Palace of the Republic* (which the Berliners called the "Ballast of the Republic") was constructed between 1973 and 1976, then closed in the fall of 1990 due to dangerously high levels of asbestos. At great expense, between 1968 and 1970, *Alexanderplatz* was expanded to twice its former size. To the west of the "Alex", the *Television Tower* was completed in 1969. New housing developments were put up in *Karl-Marx-Allee* and in *Friedrichsfelde*. In the city some elegant hotels were built, and some apartment buildings from the turn of the century in the blue collar neighborhood of the *Prenzlauer Berg* were modernized; to a great extent, however, the older buildings were completely neglected. Around 25% of the material in these buildings has deteriorated so much that the buildings can no longer be restored.

Constitution and Administration

The constitutional activity of the constitutionally elected Berlin Senate was limited to *West Berlin*. According to the city's Constitution enacted on September 1, 1950, West Berlin was until the elections of December 2, 1990, a "German State and simultaneously a city" (Art. 1) as well as a State of the Federal Republic of Germany (West Germany) (Art. 23). Because of treaty commitments in connection with the post-war occupation of the city, West Berlin's representatives to the West German Bundestag were permitted to act only in an "advisory capacity". A West German Federal law could not take effect in Berlin until the Berlin House of Representatives had formally declared it to be a Berlin law. After the end to the Allied occupation rights and the Four Power status in Berlin on October 3, 1990, federal laws now automatically take effect there.

Like Hamburg and Bremen, Berlin is a democratically governed city-state, a municipal entity with the status of a state. Legislative power here is exercised by a House of Representatives elected by the citizenry of Berlin. The members of the house in turn elect, by majority vote, the Governing Mayor (similar to the Governor of a U.S. State), the Mayor as his deputy and the 16 Senators, the equivalent of cabinet ministers. The administration of *East Berlin* had its seat in the "Red City Hall". At its head was the "Lord Mayor of Greater Berlin", supported by a city assembly. This double government continued to exist until December 2.

The basis of the Allied authority in Berlin was the London Protocol, signed by the United States, Britain, France and the Soviet Union on September 12, 1944. The city was placed under the authority of an Allied Control Council, in which all four commandants were represented, and divided into an American, British, French and Soviet sector. At the beginning of 1948, the Soviets resigned from the Allied Command, and on November 30, 1948, a separate city administration was set up in the Soviet sector, marking the division of the city.

On the map below, you see the borders of the 20 *districts* into which the city has been divided since 1920. As of 1945, twelve of these made up West Berlin and eight East Berlin. On May 20, 1979 East Berlin added a new district called Berlin-Marzahn, incorporating area taken from East Germany, a move hotly protested by the western powers. In 1985 and 1986 respectively, two further new districts came into being: Hohenschönhausen (from parts of

Weißensee*) and Hellersdorf (from parts of Marzahn*).

West Berlin	Population	sq. miles
2. Tiergarten	72,000	5.17
3. Wedding	136,702	5.66
6. Kreuzberg	127,393	3.82
7. Charlottenburg	145,564	11.15
8. Spandau	192,895	31.84
9. Wilmersdorf	180,722	12.66
10. Zehlendorf	85,161	25.98
11. Schöneberg	134,610	4.52
12. Steglitz	167,559	11.77
13. Tempelhof	162,100	14.98
14. Neukölln	276,407	16.52
20. Reinickendorf	228,971	32.90

Districts 6 and 10–14 formed the American sector, Districts 2 and 7–9 the British, and Districts 3 and 20 formed the French Sector.

East Berlin	Population	sq. miles
1. Mitte	78,952	4.13
4. Prenzlauer Berg	144,971	4.21
5. Friedrichshain	109,830	3.78
15. Treptow	102,704	15.68
16. Köpenick	111,304	49.15
17. Lichtenberg	172,277	10.19
18. Weißensee	52,484	11.62
19. Pankow	108,930	23.89
Marzahn*	170,240	12.16
Hohenschönhsn.	118,056	10.03
Hellersdorf	109,464	10.85

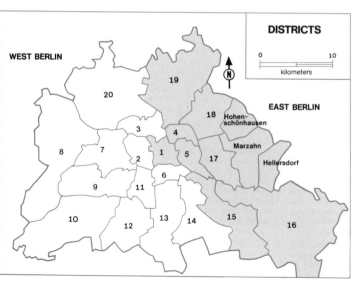

The City's History

Archaeological finds have shown that the Berlin area was populated as far back as 8,000 B.C. From the first Millennium B.C., *Swebian* tribes lived here, to be joined temporarily by Eastern Germanic *Burgunds* in the 2nd and 3rd centuries A.D. Around 650, the territory was occupied by Slavic *Wends*. The conquering of the present city of *Brandenburg* by *Henry I* in 928 began the two hundred years of conflict between Germanic and Slavic tribes for supremacy in the area.

1134 The Ascanian *Albrecht the Bear* is named Margrave of the Northern March by Emperor *Lothar;* as of 1150 A.D. he titles himself Margrave of Brandenburg.

Around 1230 The Ascanian Margraves *John I* and *Otto III* found the communities of *Cölln* and *Berlin* on the Spree – the site of today's Berlin.

1244 The first mention of Berlin on an official document (Cölln had already been mentioned in 1237).

1320 After the *Ascanians* die out, the March falls to the *Wittelsbachs*. This marks the beginning of years of battle between the cities and the landed gentry. For all this conflict, Cölln and Berlin begin to flourish economically.

1415 *Friedrich von Hohenzollern* receives both the March of Brandenburg and the title of Elector from Emperor *Sigismund.* He enters Berlin as *Frederick I.*

1442–1470 Elector *Frederick II* ends the union of Berlin and Cölln, started in 1432, and builds a castle on the Spree, which he moves into in 1470. Berlin becomes a seat of electoral authority.

1618–1648 *The Thirty Years' War* also exacts a stiff price from Berlin. The population (1618: 12,000) – further decimated by the black plague – shrinks to about half that amount by war's end.

1640–1688 *Frederick William,* the "Great Elector", sets about reconstructing and redesigning the ravaged city. He brings foreign artists to Berlin, takes in the French *Huguenots,* establishes trading companies and industrial plants, fortifies the city and connects the Elbe and Oder Rivers via the *Frederick William Canal.* The districts of *Friedrichswerder* and *Dorotheenstadt* come into being outside the fortress.

1688–1713 Elector *Frederick III,* from 1701 King *Frederick I,* continues his fa-

ther's plans with the laying out of *Friedrichstadt*. In 1710, Berlin has a population of 56,000.

1713–1740 King *Frederick William I,* the "Soldiers' King", extends the Friedrichstadt.

1740–1786 King *Frederick II the Great.* He makes Berlin into a major European capital. During his reign the population grows from 81,000 to 150,000. New cotton and silk mills go into operation around 1750, and Berlin becomes Germany's most important textile center. Starting in 1770, the *Linden* is expanded into a grand boulevard. During the *Seven Years' War,* Berlin is attacked and occupied by the Russians and the Austrians.

1786–1797 King *Frederick William II.* Berlin becomes "The City of the Enlightenment".

1797–1840 King *Frederick William III.* After the collapse of the Prussian military forces in the Battle of Jena and Auerstedt, *Napoleon I* enters Berlin on October 27, 1806; two years of French occupation begin. – In 1810 *Wilhelm von Humboldt* founds Berlin University, which soon becomes one of the most important institutes of higher learning in Germany. In 1811 *Jahn,* "Father of Sports", sets up the first German athletic field on the Hasenheide. – With the defeat of Napoleon I, the rebirth of Berlin begins. *Schinkel, Rauch* and *Lenné* design a new Berlin. – In 1838, the Berlin-Potsdam railroad connection is established, in 1839 the first horsedrawn omnibus line (Alexanderplatz to Potsdamer Platz).

1840–1861 King *Frederick William IV.* Berlin becomes one of Europe's most important industrial cities. In 1848, the population is 400,000. – On March 18, 1848, the *March Revolution* breaks out. Frederick William IV pledges his support for the unification of Germany. A (shortlived) Prussian National Assembly is convened. On April 3, 1849 Frederick William IV declines the Imperial Crown offered him by the Frankfurt Parliament.

1861–1888 King *William I* (from 1871 German Emperor). *Bismarck* becomes Prime Minister of Prussia (1862–1890). In 1867, following the victorious conclusion of the war with Austria, Berlin becomes the capital of the North German Federation, seat of the Reichstag (Parliament) and the Customs Parliament. On January 18, 1871 William I is proclaimed *German Emperor* in Versailles. Berlin becomes the capital of the German Empire. Its population has now risen to 826,000. Bismarck acts as an "honest broker" at the *Berlin Congress* of 1878, which terminates the Russo-Turkish war.

1888 Emperor *Frederick III* reigns only 99 days (from March 9 to June 15).

1888–1918 Emperor *William II*. He discharges *Bismarck* (3/20/1890). The "foundation years" bring a massive economic upswing to the city. By 1900 Berlin's population has advanced to 1,900,000. In 1902 the first subway line is opened.

11/9/1918 The *Republic* is proclaimed from the Reichstag building.

1920 Berlin is unified with its suburbs to make one single municipal unit. It now has a population of 4,100,000. During the "Weimar Republic", Berlin is the political, economic and cultural center of Germany.

1/30/1933 *Hitler* seizes power.

1936 Games of the *XIth Olympiad* in Berlin. American Jesse Owens dominates the competition and wins four gold medals.

1939–1945 *World War II*. On November 23, 1943, the steady bombardment of the national capital begins, culminating in the first land attack by Soviet forces on April 21, 1945. On May 2, 1945 the city is captured by the Red Army. On June 5, 1945, Berlin becomes the seat of the Supreme Allied Control Council. A conference of the great powers takes place in *Potsdam*. On July 4, American and British troops enter the city, followed by French forces on August 12. Berlin becomes a *four-sector city*.

1946 A democratic *City Assembly* (Social Democratic, Liberal, Social Unity [Communist] and Christian Democratic parties) is elected, both the first and last free postwar election in Berlin.

1948 Following the resignation of the Soviet Union from the Allied Control Council (3/20) and the Allied Command (6/16), the *Blockade* of the western part of the city begins (6/24). Starting on June 28, the city is supplied by the Berlin airlift. Every day almost 1,000 American and British aircraft land at the three West Berlin airfields, Tempelhof, Gatow and Tegel. – On Nov. 30, a separate *municipal government* is proclaimed in East Berlin. This seals the division of the city.

1949 Lifting of the blockade on May 12th.

– On October 7, the German Democratic Republic is founded and East Berlin declared her capital.

1950 On October 1, the new constitution of West Berlin goes into effect. The first Governing Mayor is *Ernst Reuter*.

1953 Workers' rebellion on June 17 in East Berlin is put down by force of arms.

1957 In February the Bundestag declares Berlin to be the capital of Germany. – On October 3, *Willy Brandt* becomes Governing Mayor.

1958 The Soviet "Berlin Ultimatum" of 11/27 demands the departure of the western powers from Berlin and the transformation of Berlin into a "demilitarized free city". In their reply (12/31) the western powers declare that they are not prepared to give up their rights in West Berlin.

8/13/1961 The construction of the Wall is begun. S-Bahn (metropolitan railroad) and U-Bahn (subway) connections between the two parts of the city are cut off.

1963 American President *John F. Kennedy* visits West Berlin on June 26. On the balcony of Schöneberg City Hall he makes the famous speech in which he declares: "Ich bin ein Berliner."

1972 With the conclusion of the "Berlin Agreement", West Berliners can again enter East Berlin and the G.D.R.; transit formalities between Berlin and West Germany are simplified.

1979 On July 9, the western powers protest in Moscow against a law enacted on June 28 by the G.D.R. Volkskammer (Parliament) permitting the direct election of East Berlin delegates to the Volkskammer. The allies stress the quadripartite status of Greater Berlin, which cannot be changed by one signatory.

1981 *Richard von Weizsäcker* becomes the first Christian Democratic Governing Mayor of West Berlin, to be succeeded in 1984 by *Eberhard Diepgen*.

1987/88 The city celebrates its 750th Anniversary.

1988 Berlin is designated the "Cultural Capital of Europe 1988".

1989 On November 9 the Berlin Wall is opened. On December 22 the Brandenburger Tor is reopened (for pedestrians).

1990 On October 3, Berlin is reunited. On December 2, the new House of Representatives is elected.

Art and Literature

Romanesque and Gothic

Most of the few buildings which remain from the Middle Ages were either reconstructed at a later date or destroyed in the Second World War, which is why the *Heiliggeistkapelle* (Chapel of the Holy Spirit – 13th century, see p. 59) and the simple Gothic *Marienkirche* (St. Mary's Church), are among the very few buildings of this early time worth mentioning. The latter church contains a significant work of mediaeval fresco art, the 72 foot long "Dance of Death". The restored *Nikolaikirche* (St. Nicholas' Church) in the center of the old city of Spandau also dates back to the 15th century.

Also worthy of attention are the 55 or so former village churches, most of which were begun in the 13th century: *Britz, Buckow, Dahlem, Heiligensee, Lichterfelde, Mariendorf, Marienfelde, Rudow, Schmargendorf,* etc. The oldest of these is the Romanesque village church of *Marienfelde,* built in 1192.

Renaissance

The most significant Renaissance building was torn down in the years 1950/51 – built in 1538 by *Caspar Theyss,* the former *City Palace* of the Prussian kings on an island in the Spree in the eastern section of Berlin. The many ornate private houses of that period have also disappeared – with the exception of the house built in 1624 which was the home of the *Ribbeck* family made famous by author Theodor Fontane (Breite Strasse 35 – see p. 59).

Baroque

In the Baroque period, the great architect and sculptor *Andreas Schlüter* (1664–1718) dominated Berlin's artistic life. One of the most important works of sculpture from that period is his *Equestrian Statue of the Great Elector,* which today stands in front of Charlottenburg Palace. Schlüter was also a major contributor to the expansion of the *City Palace* and the construction of the *Zeughaus* (Armory – 1695–1706). Also noteworthy was the Swedish architect *Eosander von Göthe* (ca. 1670–1695), who, together with *Johann Arnold Nering* (1659–1695), designed *Charlottenburg Palace.* Many churches built around 1700, such as the *Parochial Church,* the *German Cathedral* and the *French Cathedral* were either destroyed or badly damaged in the last war. (and rebuilt in the meantime).

Rococo

When Frederick the Great ascended the throne (1740) the Rococo era entered Berlin. Its most important master was *Georg Wenzeslaus von Knobelsdorff* (1699–1753). He built the *Opera House* on Unter den Linden, and *Sans Souci Palace,* redesigned the *Potsdam Town Palace* and added the east wing with its *Golden Gallery,* a masterwork of Prussian Rococo, to *Charlottenburg Palace.*

Frederick the Great brought many French artists to Berlin, among them the painter *Charles Amédée Vanloo.* His court painter, *Antoine Pesne* (1683–1757), had already been active in Berlin during the reign of Frederick I. Danzig painter and copper engraver *Daniel Chodowiecki* made a name for himself in his realistic depictions of his age.

As Frederick the Great only invited French authors to Berlin, a native literary culture could not become established during his reign.

Classicism and Romanticism

Classicism made its appearance around the middle of the 18th century. It would soon bring forth a number of major works of art in Berlin. The main exponents of this style were *Carl Gotthard Langhans* (1733–1808), the builder of the *Brandenburg Gate,* and *Karl Friedrich Schinkel* (1741–1841), who determined Berlin's architecture throughout the entire 19th century. Schinkel's legacy to Berlin included the *Neue Wache* (New Watch), Unter den Linden, the *"Schauspielhaus"-Theatre* on the former Gendarme Market, now the Platz der Akademie, the *Old Museum* on Museum Island, to name but a few of his more outstanding works.

The two most important sculptors of this epoch were *Gottfried Schadow* (1764–1850), who created the *Quadriga* on the Brandenburg Gate, and his pupil *Christian Daniel Rauch* (1777–1857), to whom we owe the tombs of *Queen Louise* and *Frederick William III* (in the mausoleum in the Charlottenburg palace gardens).

The outstanding painter of the Romantic era was landscape artist *Karl Blechen*

(1798–1840). Exponents of the Biedermeier period were portrait and horse painter *Franz Krüger* (1797–1857), architectural painter *Eduard Gärtner* (1801–1877) and genre painter *Theodor Hosemann* (1807–1831).

At the end of the 18th century, Berlin became a literary center for the early Romantic movement, the main exponents of which were poets and Shakespeare translators *Ludwig Tieck* (1773–1853) and *Friedrich Schlegel* (1772–1829). Their translations are largely accountable for the great master's plays being more frequently performed in Germany than anywhere else, including England. Poets *Adelbert von Chamisso* (1771–1838) and *Achim von Arnim* (1781–1831) also made major contributions to the Romantic movement. *E.T.A. Hoffmann* (1776–1822), whose life is rather freely depicted in Jacques Offenbach's fantastic opera *The Tales of Hoffmann*, was the century's ultimate renaissance man: conductor, poet, philosopher, theatre director, composer, lawyer.

Historicism

The emergence of Berlin as a world capital in the middle of the 19th century brought about an upsurge of architectural activity which took its inspiration from style forms of the Renaissance and Baroque periods. Schinkel's pupils, *Ludwig Persius* (1803–1845), *Friedrich Stüler* (1800–1865) and *Johann Heinrich Strack* (1805–1880), continued to expound their master's ideas. Among Strack's many designs were the *National Gallery* and the *Victory Column*. Other buildings dating back to this period include the *"Red" City Hall*, designed by *H. F. Waesemann* (1813–1879), the *Reichstag Building* by *Paul Wallot* (1841–1912) and the *Cathedral* at the Lustgarten by *J. Raschdorff* (1823–1914).

Amongst the sculptors, *Reinhold Begas* (1821–1911) set the tone for the creativity of the era with his Neo-Baroque style. The most significant of Berlin's painters of this period was *Adolph von Menzel* (1815–1905), who idealized the era of Frederick the Great as well as creating a number of works in the style of the period.

The critical-realistic Berlin style entered literary history with the works of *Willibald Alexis* (1798–1871), *Adolf Glassbrenner* (1810–1876) and, in particular, *Theodor Fontane* (1819–1898), whose works are still popular today. His novels have inspired many of the New German Cinema's most highly regarded films.

20th Century

The period after 1900 saw the construction of primarily functional buildings such as department stores and factories. Worthy of mention are *Hans Poelzig's* (1869–1936) *Broadcasting House* and the *Olympic Stadium*, designed by *Werner March* (1894–1976).

1900 marked the beginning of the high period of painting in Berlin. This was when such great German impressionist masters as painter and illustrator *Max Liebermann* (1847–1935), portraitist and landscape painter *Lovis Corinth* (1858–1925) and *Max Slevogt* (1868–1932), primarily renowned for his portraiture, all lived and worked here. *Käthe Kollwitz* (1867–1945) is best known for her graphics, as is *Heinrich Zille*, whose sociocritical cartoons so tellingly illustrate Berlin slum life at that time.

Like Impressionism, the Expressionistic movement, which made its appearance around 1910, had its German center in Berlin, and from here its influence spread around the world. Here, among others, worked *Emil Nolde* (1867–1956), *Max Pechstein* (1881–1955), *Karl Schmidt-Rottluff* (1884–1976), *Karl Hofer* (1878–1955), *Erich Heckel* (1883–1969), *Max Beckmann* (1884–1950) and *George Grosz* (1893–1959).

Best known of the period's sculptors were *Hugo Lederer* (1871–1938), *August Gaul* (1869–1921), *Georg Kolbe* (1877–1947) and *Fritz Klimsch* (1870–1960). *Renée Sintenis* created the "Berlin Bear", symbol of the city.

Of the hundreds of young painters and sculptors whose work has gone well beyond the Berlin city limits we can only mention a few representative names: the "Berlin Realists" *Peter Sorge, Wolfgang Petrick, Hans-Jürgen Diehl, Ulrich Baehr, Arwed Gorella*, then *Johannes Grützke, Manfred Bluth, Gerd Winner, Peter Foeller* and the sculptor *Joachim Schmettau* along with the husband and wife team *Matschinsky-Denninghoff*, whose immense pieces can be found in many Berlin streets. Many West German and foreign artists spend shorter or longer periods enlivening the Berlin art scene, many of them aided by exchange scholarships.

And the Berlin literary scene is every bit as active. Berlin is the home of such outstanding personalities as *Günter Grass, Peter Schneider, Sarah Kirsch, Elisabeth Plessen, Stefan Heym, Christa Wolf* and the dramatist *Heiner Müller*.

Getting There

By train

Trains traveling to Berlin have diners, couchette and pullman facilities and run several times a day. You can make seat or sleeper reservations through your travel agent or one of the many agencies of the German Federal Railroad throughout the world. (The New York office can be reached by writing or calling: German Federal Railroad, General Agency for North and Central America, 747 Third Avenue, 33rd Floor, New York, N.Y. 10017, tel.: 2 12/3 08-31 00.) Trains arrive and depart at the stations at the Zoologischer Garten and Berlin Hauptbahnhof; it is also possible to get on or off at the Berlin-Wannsee or Berlin-Spandau stations. From the Wannsee train station there is also a connection (more often than hourly) through Griebnitz and Babelsberg to the Potsdam Hauptbahnhof, and from the Charlottenburg S-Bahn station there is a connection via Spandau – Staaken – Dallgow – Westermark – Bredow to Nauen (18 times a day).

By plane

Berlin's *Tegel Airport* in the former western part of the city connects the city with other German cities and other countries. There are direct flights to all major West German cities and many European airports. Up until now there are no flights from Schönefeld Airport to what was formerly West Germany, but there are good connections to other European and non-European countries.

By train to Berlin

		1st Class	2nd Class
From		DM	DM
Cologne	OW	194.00	129.00
	RT	375.00*	250.00*
Frankfurt	OW	168.00	112.00
	RT	314.00*	210.00*
Hamburg	OW	95.20	63.40
	RT	175.40*	116.80*
Munich	OW	207.00	138.00
	RT	394.00*	263.00*

OW = one way; RT = round trip; prices valid as of November 1990. *Note: the prices given are for regular fares, but there are special "super saver" and ten-day return tickets to Berlin.

Flights to Berlin

		Tourist	SPR
From		DM	DM
Cologne/	OW	313.00	–
Bonn	RT	626.00	404.00
Düsseldorf	OW	313.00	–
	RT	626.00	404.00
Frankfurt	OW	291.00	–
	RT	582.00	370.00
Hamburg	OW	213.00	–
	RT	426.00	189.00
Munich	OW	336.00	–
	RT	672.00	426.00

		OW	RT
London	£	150.00	300.00
Paris	FF	1,950.00	3,900.00
Vienna	öS.	4,330.00	8,660.00
Zürich	sfr.	466.00	932.00
New York	U.S.$	983.00	1,966.00
Chicago	U.S.$	1,293.00	2,586.00
Los Angeles	U.S.$	1,325.00	2,650.00
Hamilton	Can.$	1,207.00	2,414.00

OW = one way; RT = round trip; SPR = special round trip fare. Air fares from outside Germany are all regular fares. Special reduced fares are available from many European and North American cities. Consult your travel agent for details.

In the western part of the city public transportation, including the U-Bahn, S-Bahn, and buses, is operated by the *BVG* (Berlin Transit Authority). Information about the entire BVG system is available at the customer service center in the U-Bahn station Kleistpark, Grunewaldstrasse 1 at the corner of Potsdamer Strasse. A map of the system and a schedule which includes all lines, both east and west, and is valid for six months, can be purchased for 2 DM at S- and U-Bahn stations.

The *BVB* operates the U-Bahn, S-Bahn, buses and streetcars in the eastern part of the city. Their customer service offices are at the Alexanderplatz and Warschauer Strasse S-Bahn stations.

Fares (As of November 1, 1990)

A single ticket for an unlimited number of trips within a two hour period on the U-Bahn, S-Bahn or bus costs

DM 2.70 (reduced price for children and the unemployed is DM 1.70), a multiple ride ticket (valid for 5 trips) DM 11.50 (reduced DM 7). Tickets for short distances (6 bus or 3 train stops) cost DM 1.70 (reduced DM 1.20), the "Ku'damm Ticket" (Rathenauplatz to Wittenbergplatz) costs DM 1, a 6-day ticket for the entire system (Monday though Saturday) costs DM 26. The price of the "Berlin Ticket", which is valid for an unlimited number of trips in the entire transportation network, costs DM 9 for one day (reduced DM 5). All BVG tickets (with the exception of the tickets for short distances) are valid for the entire Berlin network and for Potsdam, Schöneiche, Woltersdorf and Strausberg.

U-Bahn

There are eight lines in the western and two in the eastern section of the city.

Western section:
U 1: Schlesisches Tor – Wittenbergplatz – Zoo – Olympiastadion – Ruhleben.
U 2: Wittenbergplatz – Spichernstrasse – Dahlem-Dorf – Krumme Lanke.
U 3: Wittenbergplatz – Uhlandstraße.
U 4: Nollendorfplatz – Innsbrucker Platz.
U 6: Tegel – Leopoldplatz – Friedrichstrasse – Stadtmitte – Tempelhof – Alt-Mariendorf.
U 7: Rathaus Spandau – Bismarckstrasse – Kleistpark – Neukölln – Rudow.
U 8: Paracelsus-Bad – Osloer Strasse – Bernauer Strasse – Alexanderplatz – Jannowitzbrücke – Neukölln, Leinestrasse.
U 9: Osloer Strasse – Hansaplatz – Zoo – Kurfürstendamm – Rathaus Steglitz.

Eastern section:
Pankow (Vinetastrasse) – Alexanderplatz – Stadtmitte – Otto-Grotewohl-Strasse.
Hönow – Hellersdorf – Tierpark – Frankfurter Allee – Alexanderplatz.

There is an "Airport Transfer" from Tegel Airport to Schönefeld Airport via Ernst-Reuter-Platz – Zoo – Martin-Luther-Strasse. Its symbol is a shaded triangle.

S-Bahn

The S-Bahn (metropolitan railroad), once the most efficient means of public transportation in Berlin, has lost its former significance. The routes that are no longer active are to be improved and reopened. There are three lines in the western section:
S 1: Frohnau – Humboldthain – Unter den Linden – Anhalter Bhf. – Wannsee.
S 2: Gesundbrunnen – Unter den Linden – Yorckstrasse – Mariendorf – Lichtenrade.

S 3: Königs Wusterhausen and Erkner – Friedrichstrasse – Zoo – Wannsee.
S 3: Westkreuz – Zoo – Alexanderplatz – Plänterwald – Grünau – Schönefeld.

S-Bahn routes in the eastern section:
Alexanderplatz – Ostkreuz – Lichtenberg – Hohenschönhausen – Wartenberg.
Alexanderplatz – Ostkreuz – Lichtenberg – Marzahn – Ahrensfelde.
Oranienburg – Schönhauser Allee – Ostkreuz – Flughafen Schönefeld.
Bernau – Pankow – Ostkreuz – Grünau.
Blankenburg – Pankow – Spindlersfeld.
Buch – Warschauer Strasse – Spindlersfeld.
Friedrichstrasse – Alexanderplatz – Ostkreuz – Lichtenberg – Strausberg.

Buses

Buses run on an average of every ten minutes, more frequently during rush hours. On most buses, passengers get on in front and pay their fares to the driver. You can also cancel prepurchased tickets in cancelling machines in other parts of the bus. The most important bus lines run all night. The bus lines serving the airport are Numbers 8 and 9.

Excursions

BVG excursion buses leave from the zoo (Hardenbergplatz) for *Schildhorn, Grunewald Tower, Peacock Island (Nikolskoe);* from Wannsee for *Peacock Island (Nikolskoe);* from the Nikolassee S-Bahn station for *Wannsee Beach* and from the Tegel subway station for *Tegel Beach.* These buses operate only during excursion season (Information: Customer Service, BVG, Tel. 216 50 88).

By ship

Hourly BVG ferry service is provided between *Wannsee* and *Kladow* and *Wannsee* and *Potsdam.* A normal BVG ticket is valid for passage on these boats. In addition there are a number of privately owned shipping lines which provide service down waterways on the *Upper* and *Lower Havel, Tegel Lake* and various Berlin canals traveling through the downtown area to destinations in *Tegel* or *Peacock Island.*

You can get further information from the individual shipping lines (e.g. Reederei Riedel, Stern- und Kreisschiffahrt, Reederei Winkler). In the eastern part of the city the "Weisse Flotte" ("White Fleet") provides regularly scheduled and excursion travel on the *Havel* and the Berlin lakes. Its primary point of departure is the S-Bahn station at *Treptow* (further points of departure are *Köpenick, Neue Mühle, Grünau, Friedrichshagen*).

13

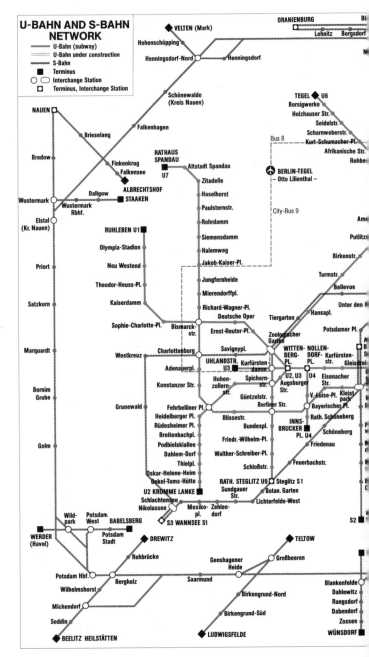

U-BAHN AND S-BAHN NETWORK

U-Bahn (subway)
U-Bahn under construction
S-Bahn
■ Terminus
◯ ⬭ Interchange Station
▢ Terminus, Interchange Station

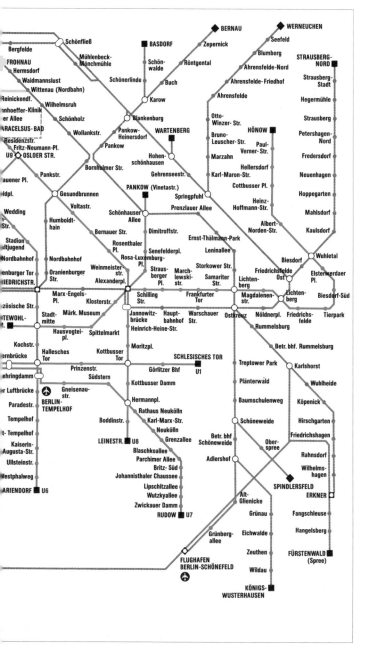

Bergfelde
Schönfließ
BASDORF
BERNAU
WERNEUCHEN
Seefeld
Mühlenbeck-Mönchmühle
Zepernick
Blumberg
STRAUSBERG-NORD
FROHNAU
Schön-walde
Röntgental
Ahrensfelde-Nord
Strausberg-Stadt
Hermsdorf
Schönerlinde
Buch
Ahrensfelde-Friedhof
Waidmannslust
Wittenau (Nordbahn)
Karow
Ahrensfelde
Hegermühle
Reinickendf.
Wilhelmsruh
nhoeffer-Klinik
er Allee
Schönholz
Blankenburg
Otto-Winzer-Str.
HÖNOW
Strausberg
ARACELSUS-BAD
Wollankstr.
Pankow-Heinersdorf
WARTENBERG
Bruno-Leuscher-Str.
Paul-Verner-Str.
Petershagen-Nord
Besidenzstr.
Fritz-Neumann-Pl.
Pankow
Hohen-schönhausen
Marzahn
Fredersdorf
U9 OSLOER STR.
Bornholmer Str.
Gehrenseestr.
Hellersdorf
Karl-Maron-Str.
Neuenhagen
auener Pl.
Pankstr.
PANKOW (Vinetastr.)
Cottbusser Pl.
Hoppegarten
ldpl.
Gesundbrunnen
Springpfuhl
Heinz-Hoffmann-Str.
Mahlsdorf
Wedding
Voltastr.
Schönhauser Allee
Prenzlauer Allee
Albert-Norden-Str.
Kaulsdorf
Humboldt-hain
Bernauer Str.
Dimitroffstr.
Str.
Stadion ltjugend
Rosenthaler Pl.
Ernst-Thälmann-Park
Biesdorf
Wuhletal
Nordbahnhof
Nordbahnhof
Rosa-Luxemburg-Pl.
Senefelderpl.
Leninallee
Friedrichsfelde Ost
Elsterwerdaer Pl.
enburger Tor
Oranienburger Str.
Weinmeister str.
Straus-berger Pl.
March-lewski-str.
Storkower Str.
Samariter Str.
Lichten-berg
IEDRICHSTR.
Alexanderpl.
Schilling Str.
Frankfurter Tor
Magdalenen-str.
Lichten-berg
Biesdorf-Süd
zösische Str.
Marx-Engels-Pl.
Klosterstr.
Jannowitz-brücke
Haupt-bahnhof
Warschauer Str.
Ostkreuz
Nöldnerpl.
Friedrichs-felde
Tierpark
TEWOHL-
.
Stadt-mitte
Märk. Museum
Heinrich-Heine-Str.
Rummelsburg
Hausvogtei-pl.
Spittelmarkt
Moritzpl.
Betr. bhf. Rummelsburg
Kochstr.
Halesches Tor
Kottbusser Tor
SCHLESISCHES TOR
Treptower Park
Karlshorst
ernbrücke
Prinzenstr.
Görlitzer Bhf
U1
ehringdamm
Südstern
Kottbusser Damm
Plänterwald
Wuhlheide
r Luftbrücke
Gneisenau-str.
Hermannpl.
Baumschulenweg
Köpenick
Paradestr.
BERLIN-TEMPELHOF
Rathaus Neukölln
Hirschgarten
Tempelhof
Boddinstr.
Karl-Marx-Str.
Schöneweide
t-Tempelhof
Neukölln
Betr. bhf Schöneweide
Friedrichshagen
Kaiserin-Augusta-Str.
LEINESTR. U8
Grenzallee
Ober-spree
Rahnsdorf
Ullsteinstr.
Blaschkoallee
Adlershof
Wilhelms-hagen
Westphalweg
Parchimer Allee
Britz-Süd
SPINDLERSFELD
ARIENDORF U6
Johannisthaler Chaussee
Lipschitzallee
Alt-Glienicke
ERKNER
Wutzkyallee
Grünau
Fangschleuse
Zwickauer Damm
RUDOW U7
Eichwalde
Hangelsberg
Grünberg-allee
Zeuthen
FÜRSTENWALD (Spree)
FLUGHAFEN BERLIN-SCHÖNEFELD
Wildau
KÖNIGS-WUSTERHAUSEN

15

Some Practical Hints

Drivers

The traffic regulations of the former G.D.R. are currently being revised to bring them into harmony with West German regulations. Although Berlin has been reunited, there are still some differences. Until the end of 1992 the law that blood alcohol levels may not be more than 0.0% will remain in force in the former G.D.R. and the eastern part of Berlin. Until the end of 1991 at intersections with an unlit green arrow, a right-turn-on-red will still be allowed. On some sections of the Autobahn, a speed limit of 100 kph (62 mph) will remain in effect until the poor road conditions are improved.

Automobile clubs in West Berlin: ADAC, Bundesallee 29, Berlin 31; AvD, Wittenbergplatz 1, Berlin 30.

Libraries

Books in English can be borrowed from the *Amerikahaus* and *British Council libraries* (see culture centers) and from the *America Commemorative Library*.

Camping sites

There are four camping sites in the western section of the city – three of these *(Kladow, Dreilinden, Haselhorst)* are open all year round, the one in *Kohlhasenbrück* is open from April 1 to September 30. All camping places must be reserved through the central office, Deutscher Camping Club e. V., Geisbergstrasse 11, D-1000 Berlin 30. The following camping sites are found in *Köpenick* in the eastern section of the city: at the *Krossinsee* (open all year round), *Zeuthener See, Grosse Krampe,* Campingplatz 1/10 between the *Langer See* and *Grosse Krampe, Kleiner Müggelsee,* and *Seddinsee* (these open only during the summer). For reservations: Servicebüro, Katzengraben 20, Köpenick O-1170 (tel. 657 14 13, 657 18 53).

Shopping

Berlin's main shopping street is the *Kurfürstendamm,* its side streets and its extension, *Tauentzienstrasse,* at the end of which you will find one of the oldest and grandest department stores in the world, the *Kaufhaus des Westens.*

Not very far away, going towards the Kurfürstendamm, you will find the *Euro-*pa Center, an American style-shopping mall with some 100 stores covering three floors, and beside it the *Mini City* (particularly interesting for younger visitors), the *Ku'damm Eck* and the *Ku'damm Karree,* together with the exclusive *Fasanen-/Uhland-passage.* On the Ku'damm's side streets you will find all kinds of shops and boutiques, selling everything from exclusive luxury items to far-out modern gear, as well as antique stores, furniture stores and art galleries (in particular on *Fasanenstrasse, Bleibtreustrasse, Schlüterstrasse, Giesebrechtstrasse* and *Pestalozzistrasse*). All told, Berlin has some 300 art galleries, most of them downtown. You will also find some of the better known bookshops on the Ku'damm, as well as the sales rooms of the State Porcelain Factory and an affiliate of Meissen Porcelain. In all, there are around 1,100 shops, with an additional 100 cafés and restaurants. Most of the ca. 250 art galleries in Berlin are also in this area.

Near *Wittenbergplatz* on *Keithstrasse* and on *Eisenacher Strasse, Motzstrasse* and on *Viktoria-Luise-Platz,* you will find the largest concentration of excellent antique shops (not to mention a number of junk shops). Every year, at the end of November and the beginning of December, the *Antiqua Berlin Fair* takes place. If you're shopping for a bargain, you'd probably be better off at some of the flea markets: the best known ones are located on the *Strasse des 17. Juni,* at the discontinued U-Bahn station at *Nollendorfplatz* and in the *Ku'damm-Karree;* you will find whole treasure troves of flea market items in the districts of Kreuzberg *(Bergmannstrasse)* and Neukölln (around *Flughafenstrasse),* as well as in Schöneberg *(Winterfeldtstrasse* and *Eisenacher Strasse).* What's more, every district has its own shopping area. The best known ones are *Schloss Strasse* in Steglitz, *Wilmersdorfer Strasse* in Charlottenburg and *Karl-Marx-Strasse* in Neukölln.

Festivals

The annual Berlin festival calendar starts with the *International Film Festival* in February, continuing on with the *Theatre Festival* in May (ten important German-language productions are invited to Berlin), the *Bach Festival* in July, the *Summer Festival* in July and August, and the renowned *Berlin Jazz Festival* at the beginning of November. The season reaches its apex with the annual *Berlin Festival Weeks* in September and October, presenting music, theatre, motion pictures and art exhibitions. The *European Film Awards* are now also held in Berlin.

Business visitors

interested in making contact with Berlin companies are cordially invited to get in touch with the *American Chamber of Commerce* at Budapester Strasse 31, Berlin 30, tel.: 2 61 55 66.

Information

about all aspects of a trip to Berlin can be acquired from the *Berlin Tourist Office (Berliner Verkehrsamt)* with main offices in the Europa Center, D-1000 Berlin 30 (open daily from 7:30 A.M.–10:30 P.M.), tel.: 2 62 60 31 (toll free from West Germany: 01 30/31 50) with information offices at Tegel Airport, at the Dreilinden border crossing point and in the Bahnhof Zoo (all open daily 8 A.M.–11 P.M.). You can get information on youth hostels from the *Youth Hostel Business Office (Geschäftsstelle)* at Tempelhofer Ufer 32, D-1000 Berlin 61, tel.: 3 05 30 55. Information on Berlin's political status is available from the *Berlin Information Center*, Hardenbergstrasse 20, D-1000 Berlin 12 (Mon.–Fri. 8–7, Sat. 8–4). For information about activities in the eastern part of Berlin, contact the Berlin Information Office at the Fernsehturm (Television Tower) (Mon. 1–6, Tues.–Fri. 8–6, Sat. and Sun. 10–6), tel 21 24 67 75 (information also available on room accommodations, theatre and concert tickets, city tours).

You can find out all about Berlin's festival activities at the *Berliner Festspiele GmbH's* "Infoladen" on Budapester Strasse 48, D-1000 Berlin 30. More information on cultural and other events, about restaurants and taverns can be found in magazines like "tip", "zitty" and "Berlin-Programm".

Consulates

United States: Clayallee 170B, Berlin 33, tel.: 8 19 50 19, 8 19 55 23.

Canada: Military Mission and Consulate, Europa Center, 12th Floor, Berlin 30, tel.: 2 61 11 61/62.

Great Britain: Uhlandstrasse 7–8, Berlin 12, tel.: 3 09 52 92/93/94, 3 09 51 46.

Allied Cultural Centers

Amerikahaus, Hardenbergstrasse 21–24, Berlin 12; *British Council*, Hardenbergstrasse 20, Berlin 12; *Maison de France*, Kurfürstendamm 211, Berlin 15. In addition to the libraries, these centers sponsor a number of political and cultural events.

Post Offices

The post office in the *Bahnhof Zoo* is open day and night. You can also pick up your general delivery mail here at the "postlagernd" window. The *Tegel Airport* post office is open daily from 6:30 A.M. to 9 P.M. You will find a post office right in the middle of the downtown area at *Marburger Strasse 12* (open weekdays from 8–6, Sat. 8–Noon).

Special issue stamps, first day covers and other philatelic items can be obtained from the *Berlin 12* post office at *Goethestrasse 2*.

Telephone

Making a phone call from west to east and vice versa is still a test of patience. Although the telephone lines have already increased threefold, of course the number of calls being made has increased even more. The area code needed to call from the western to the eastern part of the city is 0372, the area code for Potsdam is 037 33.

City tours

Several organizations conduct city tours and trips through Berlin and outlying areas daily. Departures are primarily from the corner of Kurfürstendamm and Meinekestrasse, with some also from the corner of Unter den Linden and Universitätsstrasse (at the Staatsbibliothek). The Long Tour of all Berlin (3 ½ hours) costs DM 36, the Short Tour (2 hours) DM 22. A Night Club Tour (Sat. only) costs DM 108 (4 ½ hours) or DM 90 (3 ½ hours), a trip to Potsdam (daily, 4 hours) DM 49 or DM 99 (3 times a week, 9 hours), a trip in the Spreewald (several times a week during the summer only, 6 hours) DM 49, a tour of the Havel lakes (daily during the summer, 3 ½ hours) DM 32. Berlin shipping companies offer trips to the Müggelsee (from Hansabrücke, Kongresshalle, Kottbusser Brücke).

The Berlin Tourist Office can also supply visitors with private guides, who charge about DM 100.00 for a three to four hour tour.

Accommodations

HOTELS

At the present time Berlin has a hotel capacity of about 33,000 rooms, with about 8000 of the rooms in the eastern section.

Near Kurfürstendamm and Berlin Mitte:

♛♛♛ Luxury: "Bristol Hotel Kempinski", Kurfürstendamm 27, Berlin 15. "Inter-Continental", Budapester Strasse 2, Berlin 30. "Grand Hotel", Friedrichstrasse 158, Mitte. "Metropol", Friedrichstrasse 150–153, Mitte. "Palasthotel", Karl-Liebknecht-Strasse 3, 1020 Berlin.

♛♛♛ "Ambassador", Bayreuther Strasse 42, Berlin 30. "Hotel Berlin", Lützowplatz 17, Berlin 30. "Grand Hotel Esplanade", Lützowufer 15, Berlin 30. "Mondial", Kurfürstendamm 47, Berlin 15. "Palace", Budapester Strasse (im Europa-Center), Berlin 30. "Penta", Nürnberger Strasse 65, Berlin 30. "Savoy", Fasanenstrasse 9–10, Berlin 12. "Schweizerhof", Budapester Strasse 21–31, Berlin 30. "Steigenberger", Los-Angeles-Platz 1, Berlin 30. "Berolina", Karl-Marx-Allee 31, 1020 Berlin. "Stadt Berlin", Alexanderplatz, 1026 Berlin. "Unter den Linden", Unter den Linden 14, 1080 Berlin.

♛♛ "Agon", Xantener Strasse 4, Berlin 15. "Alsterhof", Augsburger Strasse 5, Berlin 30. "Askanischer Hof", Kurfürstendamm 53, Berlin 15. "Astoria", Fasanenstrasse 2, Berlin 12. "Avantgarde", Kurfürstendamm 14–15, Berlin 15. "Berlin Excelsior", Hardenbergstrasse 14, Berlin 12. "Berlin Plaza", Knesebeckstrasse 63, Berlin 15. "Hotel Bremen", Bleibtreustrasse 25, Berlin 15. "Hotel City", Kurfürstendamm 173, Berlin 15. "Hotel Consul", Knesebeckstrasse 8–9, Berlin 12. "Curator Hotel Berlin", Grolmanstrasse 41–43, Berlin 12. "Domus", Uhlandstrasse 49, Berlin 15. "Frauenhotel Artemisia", Brandenburgische Strasse 18, Berlin 31. "Frühling am Zoo", Kurfürstendamm 17, Berlin 15. "Hamburg", Landgrafenstrasse 4, Berlin 30. "Hecker's Hotel", Grolmanstrasse 35, Berlin 12. "Kurfürstendamm am Adenauerplatz", Kurfürstendamm 68, Berlin 15. "Pientka", Kurfürstendamm 12, Berlin 15. "President", An der Urania 16–18, Berlin 30. "Residenz Berlin", Meinekestrasse 9, Berlin 15. "Sylter Hof", Kurfürstendamm 116, Berlin 30.

♙ "Atlanta", Fasanenstraße 74, Berlin 15. "Auberge", Bayreuther Straße 10, Berlin 30. "Börse", Kurfürstendamm 34, Berlin 15. "Bogota", Schlüterstraße 45, Berlin 15. "Savigny", Brandenburgische Strasse 21, Berlin 31. "Sachsenhof", Motzstrasse 7, Berlin 30. "Pension Iris", Uhlandstrasse 33, Berlin 15. "Pension Knesebeck", Knesebeckstrasse 86, Berlin 12.

Near the Exhibition Site at the Broadcasting Tower:

♛♛♛ "Seehof", Lietzenseeufer 11, Berlin 19.

♛♛ "Am Studio", Kaiserdamm 80/81, Berlin 19. "An der Oper", Bismarckstrasse 100, Berlin 12. "Hotel Brandies", Kaiserdamm 27, Berlin 19. "Hotel v. Korff", Kaiserdamm 29, Berlin 19. "Villa Kastania", Kastanienallee 20, Berlin 19.

Hotels in the Countryside:

♛♛♛ "Schloßhotel Gehrhus", Brahmsstrasse 4–10, Berlin 33.

♛♛ "Forsthaus Paulsborn", Am Grunewaldsee, Berlin 33. "Haus Bismarck", Bismarckallee 3, Berlin 33. "Landhaus Schlachtensee", Bogotastrasse 9, Berlin 37. "Wannseeblick", Königstrasse 3b/4, Berlin 39.

♙ "Diana" (Pension), Wernerstrasse 14a, Berlin 33. "Hotelpension Diana am See", Königsallee 40, Berlin 33. "Hotelpension Hagen", Hagenstrasse 50, Berlin 33. "Müggelsee", am Grossen Mügelsee, Köpenick.

Potsdam

♛♛♛ "Potsdam", Lange Brücke.
♛♛ "Am Jägertor", Am Jägertor. "Cecilienhof", Neuer Garten.

For young people:

Young visitors to Berlin are reminded that only holders of a Youth Hostel pass are entitled to the use of the hostels. You can get more information on this from the Youth Hostel Business Office, Tempelhofer Ufer 32, D-1000 Berlin 61.

JH (YH) Ernst Reuter, B 28, Hermsdorfer Damm 48–50. Jugendgästehaus, B 30, Kluckstrasse 3. Jugendgästehaus, B 38, Badeweg 1. Jugendgästehaus am Zoo, B 12, Hardenbergstrasse 9a. Studentenhotel, B 62, Meininger Str. 10. Studentenhotel Hubertusallee, B 33, Delbrückstrasse 24.

Where and What to Eat and to Drink

Berlin cuisine

Berlin's native culinary art is – let's be honest – nothing to write home about, especially if you hail from New Orleans or Quebec, but it is a good example of solid, substantial German cooking.

Typical Berlin dishes are *Eisbein* (pickled ham hocks) *with sauerkraut and mashed peas, Rinderbrust* (boiled brisket of beef) and *Kasseler Rippenspeer* (smoked pork chops). Other specialties include *Buletten* (meat balls – eaten cold with ketchup or hot with mustard) and *Hackepeter* (raw beef, pork and onions ground together). The best-known Berlin meat dish is called *Leber Berliner Art* (Berlin-style liver) everywhere but in Berlin – here it is simply called *Leber mit Apfel und Zwiebeln* (liver with apple and onions), which is what it is. The *Berliner Pfannkuchen* is not a pancake, but a savory jelly doughnut.

Berliners also go for simple, hearty beverages – the staple is beer, and the local specialty is *Berliner Weisse mit Schuss,* a white malt beer with a dollop of fruit syrup – a refreshing summer drink. Berliners also enjoy a shot of *Korn,* clear grain spirits somewhat similar to and just as potent as straight vodka.

Where to go

The western section of Berlin boasts about 5,000 restaurants, bars, cafés, pastry shops (most pastry shops serve coffee, cakes and pies to customers at tables), taverns and delightful country restaurants on the outskirts of town – no German city has more. (The eastern section of Berlin, by comparison, has about 1,300 such establishments.)

All restaurants not specifically classed as exclusive are called *Kneipen* (taverns), and there's one on practically every corner. The most authentic corner taverns (similar to bar & grill combinations in America) are to be found in the districts of Schöneberg (here Leydicke at Mansteinstr. 4 deserves special mention), Neukölln, Kreuzberg and Charlottenburg, as well as in Moabit and Wedding.

There is a huge selection of first class restaurants, with Rockendorf's Restaurant and An der Rehwiese – both Michelin one star restaurants – at the top of the list. As

Berlin has no legal closing times, a lot of people do not eat till relatively late.

Although most restaurants and taverns are not open day and night, virtually every place is open until two in the morning, and many close at four or five, or even later. This is when the "breakfast taverns" open their doors, offering hearty breakfast to help us face the day.

Berlin never goes to sleep. There is plenty of life on her streets throughout the day and night, and not just in the downtown area. Berlin's night life is so diverse, so original, naughty and attractive that tourists come from all over the world to enjoy a "pub crawl" through the streets of this city. We can only provide a small selection of the best-known Berlin night spots.

In the eastern part of the city there are relatively few restaurants. Most of them are concentrated in the Nikolaiviertel, around Alexanderplatz, on Friedrichstrasse, Unter den Linden, and at Platz der Akademie. Among the best restaurants are the Ganymed on Schiffbauerdamm, the Forellenquintett in the Grand Hotel on Friedrichstrasse and the Ermeler-Haus on the Märkisches Ufer.

Restaurants

The following restaurants are along Kurfürstendamm or nearby; the name of the district is given for those that are further away.

International cuisine:

Alt-Berliner Schneckenhaus, Kurfürstendamm 37 (garden house).
Alt-Luxemburg, Pestalozzistrasse 70.
An der Rehwiese, Nikolassee, Matterhornstrasse 101.
Bamberger Reiter, Regensburger Str. 7.
Chalet Corniche, Königsallee.
Conti-Fischstuben, Bayreuther Strasse 42 (in the Hotel Ambassador).
Da Antonio, Rankestrasse 26.
Du Pont, Budapester Strasse 1.
Grille, Kurfürstendamm/corner of Knesebeckstrasse.
Hardy an der Oper, Zauritzweg 9/corner of Bismarckstrasse.
Hemingway's, Grunewald, Hagenstrasse 18.
Kempinski, Kurfürstendamm 27.
Mövenpick in the Europa-Center.
Rockendorfs, Frohnau, Düsterhauptstrasse 1.

German and traditional Berlin cuisine:

Beiz, Schlüterstrasse 38.
Die Nolle, U-Bahn station, Nollendorfplatz.
Hardtke, Meinekestrasse 26 & 27, and in Grunewald, Hubertusallee 48.
Hecker's Deele, Grolmanstrasse 35.
Heinz Holl, Damaschkestrasse 26.
Heinz Kardell, Gervinusstrasse 24.
Mommsen-Eck, Mommsenstrasse 45.
Museumskneipe im Martin-Gropius-Bau, Stresemannstrasse 110 (Kreuzberg).
Schultheiß, Kurfürstendamm/corner Meinekestrasse.
Spree-Athen, Leibnizstrasse 60.
Tafelrunde (the "round table", specializing in mediaeval style dinners), Wilmersdorf, Nachodstrasse 21.
Weißbierstube im Berlin-Museum, Lindenstrasse 14 (Kreuzberg).

Specialty restaurants

There is hardly any kind of national cuisine not represented somewhere in Berlin.

Argentine:

Churrasco, Kurfürstendamm 177 and 214 (2 restaurants).
Los Indios, Xantener Strasse 9.
Maredo, Kurfürstendamm 48.

Austrian/Czech:

Exil, Paul-Lincke-Ufer 44a.
Zlata Praha, Meinekestrasse 4.

Chinese:

Hongkong, Kurfürstendamm 210.
Lee-Wah, Kurfürstendamm 92.
Tai Shan, Meinekestrasse 7.

Danish:

Kopenhagen, Kurfürstendamm 203.

French:

Avec, Mommsenstrasse 42.
Coq d'or, Dahlmannstrasse 20.
La Puce, Schillerstrasse 20.
Paris-Bar, Kantstrasse 152.
Paris-Moskau, Moabit, Alt-Moabit 141.

Greek:

Akropolis, Wielandstrasse 38.
Fofi, Fasanenstrasse 70.
Lissos, Pfalzburger Strasse 83.
Tatavla, Mommsenstrasse 10.
Taverna Plaka, Joachimstaler Strasse 14.

Indian:

Ashoka Taj, Leibnizstrasse 62.
Kalkutta, Bleibtreustrasse 17.

Indonesian:

Bali, Otto-Suhr-Alle 25.

Hollandstübl, Martin-Luther-Strasse 11.
Java, Nestorstrasse 6.

Italian:

Anselmo, Damaschkestrasse 17.
Bacco (Tuscan food), Marburger Strasse 5.
Borbone, Windscheidstrasse 14.
Il Faro, Schlüterstrasse 60.
La Cascina, Grunewald, Delbrückstrasse 28.
Ponte Vecchio, Spielhagenstrasse 3.
Savoia, Windscheidstrasse 31.

Japanese:

Daitokai, Europa-Center.
Sapporo Kan, Schlüterstrasse 52.

Kosher:

Ritual restaurant in the Jewish Community Center. Fasanenstrasse 79–80.

Polish:

Krakowiak, Nürnberger Strasse 14.

Portuguese:

El Pulpo, Schlüterstrasse 60.
Lusiada, Kurfürstendamm 135.

Russian:

Mazurka (night club featuring Russian specialties), Lietzenburger Strasse 74.

Spanish:

Borriquito, Wielandstrasse 6.
El Bodegon, Schlüterstrasse 61.
La Bodega, Wielandstrasse 37.

Swiss:

Auf dem Churfirsten, Ku'damm 165.
Chalet Suisse, Königin-Luise-Strasse in the Grunewald (close to the Grunewaldsee).
Tessiner Stuben, Bleibtreustrasse 33.

Turkish/Kurdish:

Istanbul, Knesebeckstrasse 77.
Kurdistan, Kaiser-Friedrich-Strasse 41. (Berlin has a huge Turkish population, and the streets in many parts of town – Kreuzberg especially – are lined with little Turkish hole-in-the-wall restaurants where the food is inexpensive and wonderful.)

Vegetarian:

Hakuin, Martin-Luther-Strasse 1.
Sim Salat, Ansbacher Strasse 11.

Yugoslavian:

Adriatic Grill, Kurfürstendamm 96.
Boka, Fasanenstrasse 73.

Friedrichstrasse – Alexanderplatz –
Nikolaiviertel

Ephraim Palais, at the Mühlendamm.
Ermelerhaus, Märkisches Ufer 12.
Ganymed, Schiffbauerdamm 5.
Grand Hotel, Friedrichstrasse 158 (international cuisine, cafés).
Hotel Berolina, Karl-Marx-Allee 31 (international cuisine, roof garden).
Hotel Stadt Berlin, Alexanderplatz (international cuisine).
La Habana, in the Hotel Metropol, Friedrichstrasse 150.
Offenbach-Stuben, Stubbenkammerstr. 8.
Operncafé, Unter den Linden 5 (wine restaurant, café and dancing).
Palasthotel, Karl-Liebknecht-Strasse (international cuisine, Asiatic restaurant, grill, café).
Reblaus, Gaudystrasse 2.
"Ribbeck-Keller", Breitestrasse 35 (international cuisine).
Zum Nußbaum, Am Nußbaum.
Zum Paddenwirt, Nikolaikirchplatz 6.
Zur letzten Instanz, Waisenstrasse 5 (historical-traditional Berlin restaurant).
Zur Rippe, Mühlendamm.

Country inns

Blockhaus Nikolskoe, Wannsee.
Café Liebig, Grünau, Regattastrasse 158.
Forsthaus Paulsborn, on Grunewaldsee.
Grunewaldturm, Havelchaussee.
Historische Gaststätte Zitadellenschänke, Spandau, at Juliusturm.
Lindwerder, on Lindwerder Island in the Havel, Havelchaussee.
Müggelseeperle, on Grosser Müggelsee.
Müggelturm, in the Müggelberg Hills.
Neu-Helgoland, on Kleiner Müggelsee, Odernheimer Strasse.
Pavillon Stölpchensee, Kohlhasenbrück.
Rübezahl, on Großer Müggelsee.
Schildhorn, Am Schildhorn 4.
Strandbaude, on Gross-Glienickersee.
Teufelssee, in the Müggelberg Hills.
Toulouse, in Forsthaus Tegel, on Tegeler See.
Wannsee-Terrassen, next to the Wannsee swimming area.
Zenner, Treptow, Alt-Treptow 14–17.

Cafés

Am Neuen See, Lichtensteinallee.
Bristol, Kurfürstendamm 35.
Huthmacher, Hardenbergstrasse 39.
Kempinski, Kurfürstendamm 27.
Kranzler, Kurfürstendamm 18/19.
Krumme, Joachimstaler Strasse 41.

Leysieffer, Kurfürstendamm 218.
Möhring, Kurfürstendamm/corner Uhlandstrasse; Kurfürstendamm/Adenauerplatz; Kurfürstendamm 234.
Mövenpick, Europa-Center.
Tasty, Kurfürstendamm.

Friedrichstrasse – Alexanderplatz

Am Marstall, Rathausstrasse, am Nikolai-Viertel.
Arkade, Französische Strasse 25.
Lindencorso, Unter den Linden 17.
Operncafé, Unter den Linden.
Pressecafé, Karl-Liebknecht-Strasse 29.
Raabediele, Märkisches Ufer 10–12, Marx-Engels-Forum.
Telecafé in the Television Tower (maximum stay – 1 hour).

Bars with music

(covering everything from rock bands to political satire)

Café EinStein (literary café, poetry readings, top quality music: Viennese atmosphere, good food), Kurfürstenstrasse 58.
Eierschale, Podbielskiallee 50 in the Landhaus Dahlem, and Rankestrasse 1.
Flöz, Nassauische Strasse 37.
Go-In, Bleibtreustrasse 17.
Joe am Ku'damm, Kurfürstendamm 225.
Nashville, Breitenbachplatz 8.
Quasimodo, Kantstrasse 12a.
Sudhaus Moabit, Stromstrasse 11.

Bars, Night Clubs and discos

The ones marked with an asterisk (*) welcome all ages. The others are primarily for young people.

Annabell's*, Fasanenstrasse 64.
Big Apple, Bundesallee 13/14.
Big Eden, Kurfürstendamm 202.
Chez Alex*, Kurfürstendamm 160.
Chez nous* (transvestite show), Marburger Strasse 14.
Dollywood* (transvestite show), Kurfürstenstrasse 114–116 (in the Sylter Hof).
Dorett*, Fasanenstrasse 74.
First, Joachimstaler Strasse 15.
I-Punkt, Europa-Center.
Irish Pub, Europa-Center.
Kudorf, Joachimstaler Strasse 15 (22 taverns in the cellar).
La vie en rose* (good variety show), in the Europa-Center.
Metropol (super disco for 3,000 people, often the site of famous band concerts), Nollendorfplatz 5.
New Eden*, Kurfürstendamm 71.
Schatulle*, Fasanenstrasse 39.

Theatres

Visitors always enjoy an evening at the opera, where the language is a secondary consideration. There are three opera houses of world renown in Berlin and plenty of concert and recital activity. Theatre lovers would do well to pay a visit to one of the drama theatres as well. The performing arts in Central Europe are considered cultural institutions like schools and libraries, and are thus handsomely subsidized. With no need to make a profit – the taxpayer has contributed 80 % and more of the price of your ticket – European theatres are free to try daring pieces and new, sometimes far-out approaches which would be impossible in a commercial theatre situation. The results are often exciting and well worth seeing, even if you don't speak German – try a classical or modern play you know well and see how it looks through the eyes of another culture. More theatre information on p. 17.

Theatres in Berlin

Deutsche Oper Berlin, Bismarckstrasse 34–37, one of the world's great opera and ballet theatres. A large number of prominent American and British artists are regular members of the ensemble.

Friedrichstadtpalast, Friedrichstrasse 107. Vaudeville theatre and the intimate "das Ei" ("the egg").

Deutsche Staatsoper, Unter den Linden 7. Magnificent performances in one of the most beautiful theatres in the world – the acoustics here are like sitting inside a cello. Chamber opera and concert presentations are given here in the Apollo-Saal.

Komische Oper, Behrenstrasse 55–57. The late Walter Felsenstein's provocative opera and operetta theatre, breathtakingly intricate and honest productions.

Schillertheater, Bismarckstrasse 110. Germany's Old Vic, old and new classics.

Schiller-Theater Werkstatt, Bismarckstrasse 110. Experimental theatre.

Schlosspark-Theater, Schloss Strasse 48. Primarily modern drama.

Berliner Ensemble, Bertolt Brecht Platz – specializing in authentic productions of Brecht's works.

Deutsches Theater und Kammerspiele, Schumannstrasse 13a. Main drama repertory theatre. Once the artistic home of Viennese director Max Reinhardt, whose faithful yet innovative interpretations of the great classics set styles on both sides of the Atlantic.

Freie Volksbühne, Schaperstrasse 24. Old and new classics.

Metropol-Theater, across the street from the Friedrichstrasse Railroad Station, operettas and musicals.

Renaissance-Theater, Hardenbergstrasse 6. Old and new classics.

Schaubühne am Lehniner Platz, Kurfürstendamm 153. One of the world's most respected experimental stages (three performances simultaneously on three ultramodern stages).

Theater am Kurfürstendamm, Kurfürstendamm 206. Drawing room comedy.

Theater des Westens, Kantstrasse 12. Broadway Musicals, Operetta.

Concerts

Philharmonie and Kammermusiksaal, Kemperplatz. Home of the world-famous Berlin Philharmonic Orchestra; musical director: Claudio Abbado.

Schauspielhaus Berlin, Mitte, Platz der Akademie.

Grosser Sendesaal des SFB, Masurenallee 8. Home of the Berlin Radio Symphony Orchestra.

Konzertsaal der Hochschule der Künste, Hardenbergstrasse 33.

Neuer Vortragssaal in der Staatsbibliothek, Potsdamer Strasse 35.

Philharmonic Hall and Reichstag Building

Museums and Galleries

Bauhaus-Archiv, Museum of Design, Tiergarten, Klingelhöfer Strasse 14, daily exc. Tues., 11–5, Fr. 11–8.

*Berlin Museum, Kreuzberg, Lindenstrasse 14, Tues.–Sun., 10 A.M.–10 P.M.

Berliner Post- und Fernmeldemuseum (Berlin Postal and Telecommunications Museum), Schöneberg, in the Urania. Mon.–Thurs. 9–5, Sat. and Sun. 10–5.

Bertolt-Brecht-Haus (Bertolt Brecht House), Mitte, Chausseestrasse 125, where playwright Bertolt Brecht lived and worked. Tues.–Fri., 10–12, Thurs. also 5–7, Sat., 9:30–2.

Botanisches Museum (Botanical Museum), Dahlem, Königin-Luise-Str. 6–8, Tues.–Sun. 10–5.

Bröhan Museum, Charlottenburg, Schloss Strasse 1a (glass, porcelain, ceramics, etc., Jugendstil and Art Deco). Tues.–Sun., 10–6.

*Brücke Museum, Dahlem, Bussardsteig 9, daily except Tues., 11–5.

Deutsches Historisches Museum (German Historical Museum), in the former Museum für Deutsche Geschichte (Museum of German History), Mitte, Unter den Linden 2. Changing exhibits. Mon.–Thurs. 9–6, Sun. 10–5.

Deutsches Rundfunkmuseum (German Radio Museum), at the Broadcasting Tower, Wed.–Mon., 10–5.

Georg-Kolbe-Museum, Charlottenburg, Sensburger Allee 25, daily, except Mon., 10–5.

Käthe-Kollwitz-Museum, Charlottenburg, Fasanenstrasse 24, daily exc. Tues., 11–6.

Kunstbibliothek Berlin (Art Library), Charlottenburg, Jebensstrasse 2 (Zoo Station). Mon., Thurs., 9–8; Fr. 9–6.

*Kunstgewerbemuseum (Museum of Applied Arts), Tiergarten, Tiergartenstrasse 6, Tues.– Fri 9–5, Sat. and Sun. 10–5.

*Kunstgewerbemuseum (Museum of Applied Arts) in Köpenick Palace, Wed.–Sun., 10–6.

*Märkisches Museum, Mitte, Am Köllnischen Park 5. Wed–Fri. 10–5, Sat. and Sun. 10–6.

Martin-Gropius-Bau (Martin Gropius Building), Kreuzberg, Stresemannstr. 110 (Berlin Gallery, Archives of the artists' association, Jewish section, changing exhibits). Tues.–Sun. 10 A.M.–10 P.M.

**Museen Dahlem (Dahlem Museums): ****Painting Gallery, Copperplate Engraving Collection, Sculpture Gallery, Ethnological Museum, Museum of East Asian Art, Museum of Islamic Art, Museum of Indian Art), in Dahlem, Arnimallee 23–27 and Lansstrasse 8. Tues.–Fri. 9–5, Sat. and Sun. 10–5.

*Museen im Schloss Charlottenburg (Museums in Charlottenburg Palace): Egyptian Museum, Museum of Antiquities and Treasure Room, Museum of Prehistory and Early History), Luisenplatz and Schloss Strasse 1 and 70, Mon.–Thurs. 9–5 Sat. and Sun. 10–5, closed Fri. Historical rooms in the palace, daily, exc. Mon., 10–5, Thurs. 10–8.

Museum für Deutsche Volkskunde (German Ethnological Museum,), Dahlem, Im Winkel 6. Open the same times as the Dahlem Museums.

*Museum für Naturkunde (Natural History Museum), Mitte, Invalidenstrasse 43. Tues. – Sun., 9:30–5.

Museum für Verkehr und Technik (Communication, Transportation and Technology Museum), Kreuzberg, Trebbiner Strasse 9. Tues.– Fri. 9–6, Sat. and Sun., 10–6.

**Museumsinsel (Museum Island: Old Museum with New Divison of the National Gallery, Copperplate Engraving Exhibition; Bode-Museum with Egyptian Museum, Painting Gallery, Sculpture Collection, Numismatic Collection, Early Christian-Byzantine Collection, Museum of Prehistory and Early History, National Gallery, ****Pergamon Museum* with collection of Antiquities, East Asian Collection, Ethnological Museum, Near Eastern and Islamic Museum). Wed. – Sun. 10–6 (Near Eastern Museum and Pergamon Altar also Mon./Tues. 10–6).

*Musikinstrumentenmuseum (Musical Instruments Museum), Tiergarten, Tiergartenstrasse 1. Tues.–Fri. 9–5, Sat. and Sun. 10–5.

*Nationalgalerie (National Gallery), Tiergarten, Potsdamer Strasse 50. Tues.–Fri. 9–5, Sat. and Sun. 10–5.

*Otto-Nagel-Haus (Otto Nagel House), Mitte, Märkisches Ufer 16–18. Sun.–Thurs., 10–6.

Postmuseum (Postal Museum), Mitte, Leipziger/Ecke Mauerstrasse. Tues.–Sat., 10–6.

Walk 1: Zoo District and Kurfürstendamm

Our walk begins at Berlin's centrally located *Bahnhof Zoologischer Garten,* the western part of the city's largest long distance train station. Here you can transfer to the S-Bahn or U-Bahn, and this is also the starting point of a number of different bus lines as well as BVG excursion tours. For many years, this station was a source of embarrassment for the city, a kind of gathering place for drop-outs of all kinds, set against the dark background of what can only be called a ruin. There were reasons for this. For a long time, the entire station was the property of the G. D. R., and the government of that country refused to allow any restoration work to be done on the building. When the S-Bahn passed over to BVG ownership in 1984, work began almost immediately on refurbishing that part of the station, and the G.D.R. finally gave permission for an overhaul, which was completed in 1987.

Across the street from the Bahnhof Zoo is one of the entrances to the zoological gardens: the other one, the ornate "Elephant Gate", recently restored to its pre-war glory, can be found on *Budapester Strasse.* This is also the direct entry to the aquarium.

Russian Log Building in the "Zoo"

Visitors' favorites include Germany's only giant panda. In the *monkey house* you will find a large quantity of breeding stock, including gorillas, orang-utans, proboscis monkeys, and many others. The *rhinoceros* and *elephant houses* are also well worth a visit. The old trees, beautiful green lawns, ponds and brooks make the zoo a perfect place for an excursion (restaurants, playgrounds).

**Zoologischer Garten [1]

Open daily from 9–7 (Sun., from 8). Admission DM 7.50, children from 3–15 DM 4.00. Combination zoo and aquarium ticket DM 11.50 for adults, DM 6.00 for children.

> The zoo (82 acres), laid out in 1841, is German's oldest and the ninth zoo to be established in the world (after Vienna, Paris, London, Dublin, Bristol, Manchester, Amsterdam and Antwerp). It was almost completely destroyed in a bombardment on November 23, 1943 – only 91 animals survived. Today, with approximately 11,000 mammals and birds, representing some 1,600 different species, it has one of the most extensive animal collections in the world.

One particular point of attraction is the *wild animal house,* with the largest open air enclosure in the world, and a fascinating subterranean section featuring night animals. The modern *bird house* is Europe's largest and there is nothing anywhere to compare with the huge *open air bear enclosures.*

**Aquarium

Open daily from 9–6, the last Saturday in the month 9 A.M.–9 P.M. Admission DM 7.00 for adults, DM 3.50 for children.

The aquarium, built in 1913 and handsomely expanded in 1980, is Europe's largest. It contains around 8,520 individual creatures representing some 600 different species, which also makes it one of the most extensive collections of species in the world. Whole natural landscapes are on display, complete with rivers, fish, amphibians, etc.; here, in faithful reproductions of their natural habitats, you will find crocodiles and alligators. The *insectarium* houses arthropods from all over the world. Near the Aquarium, at Budapester Strasse 44, we find the *Staatliche Kunsthalle Berlin* (State Art Gallery), renowned for its exhibitions.

*Kaiser-Wilhelm-Gedächtniskirche [2]

The Emperor William Memorial church was constructed between 1891 and 1895 by Franz Schwechten in Neoromanesque style as a memorial to Emperor William I and commemorates the establishment of the German Empire by Bismarck and his emperor. The church was badly damaged in World War II. For years afterwards there was a great debate over whether the church should be restored or torn down, and this was finally settled with a compromise: the 207 foot ruined tower (the locals call it the "hollow tooth") was preserved, in the middle of an otherwise modern building complex, as a warning reminder of the ravages of war.

The ensemble of buildings, designed by Egon Eiermann and put up between 1959 and 1961, consists of an octagonal central structure, a small chapel and a hexagonal church tower (175 ft.). The walls of the central building are divided into 300 small squares inlaid with stained glass mosaics from Chartres. The melody played by the carillon in the tower ruins was composed by Prince Louis Ferdinand of Prussia.

Eiermann's creation also aroused a storm of controversy both pro and con: the Berliners called it a "silo for souls". Even today this most symbolic building is again in the news: the ruined tower is likely to cave in at any time, and the concrete beehive structure needs to be restored.

Emperor William Memorial Church

Europa-Center [3]

Berlin's largest shopping mall, office complex and amusement center was opened in 1965. It contains around 100 shops, cafés, bars and restaurants, five motion picture theatres, the "Stachelschweine" cabaret, the Palace Hotel, the "Spielbank Berlin" gambling casino (roulette, baccara, black jack; daily from 3:00 P.M. to 3:00 A.M.), the revue theatre

"La vie en rose", the "thermals" (saunas) and many other features. This is also where the Berlin tourist office is located. One very rewarding experience is the view from the 20th floor (observation deck). The "little casino" (100 slot machines) can be found in the Hotel Steigenberger (see p. 18).

A new, much admired attraction was opened on the Europa Center's ground floor in May of 1982: the *clock of flowing time,* a 43-foot tall water clock, designed by the French physicist Gitton for people who don't really need a timepiece but would rather marvel at the spectacle of

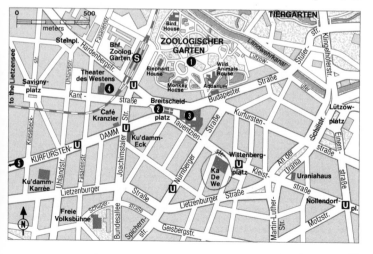

time in its flow. In 1984 another major attraction was opened outside the Europa Center: *Joachim Schmettau's "World Fountain", opened in 1984* and known locally as the "water dumpling".

Heading west from Breitscheidplatz, we start down *Kantstrasse,* which, along with its extension *Neue Kantstrasse,* cuts through the Charlottenburg district, leading to the International Congress Center (see p. 34). In the right, shortly before you get to *Fasanenstrasse,* you will find the *Theater des Westens* [4], built in 1895/96 and recently very successfully restored.

After this comes *Savignyplatz,* one of the city's tavern paradises (you'll even find a couple in the S-Bahn arches), and the city's "alternative" bookshop section, where a number of rare books and books in foreign languages are sold.

Behind *Wilmersdorfer Strasse,* Charlottenburg's main shopping street, Neue Kantstrasse, cuts through the idyllic *Lietzenseepark,* 25 acres of greensward surrounding a lake (restaurant, rowboat rental). The street ends at the *Messedamm* with the International Congress Center.

Leading eastward from Breitscheidplatz is the extension of the Kurfürstendamm, *Tauentzienstrasse,* one of Berlin's principal shopping streets, running from here to *Wittenbergplatz* in Schöneberg, where you will find one of Europe's most lavish department stores, the *Kaufhaus des Westens* (KaDeWe). Its renowned grocery and delicatessen department, one of the largest in the world, is an absolute must.

The street continues on across *Kleiststrasse,* to the discontinued *Nollendorfplatz* U-Bahn station. Here a collection of antique dealers sell their wares in 16 erstwhile subway cars. The flea market, with the *Zille Museum,* is open daily, except Tuesdays, from 11 to 7. Kleiststrasse is also the address of the *Uraniahaus,* with the *Post- und Fernmeldemuseum* (Postal and Telecommunication Museum).

*Kurfürstendamm

This was once a corduroy road, where the Electors (Kurfürsten) rode from their residence on the Spree Island to the hunting grounds in the Grunewald. It wasn't until 1886 that the road was made into a proper paved road on orders from Bismarck.

Of the some 250 buildings lining the two or so miles of the Kurfürstendamm to the Halensee Bridge, 200 were destroyed or severely damaged in World War II. Most of them have since been replaced by newer buildings, not all of which are architectural masterpieces. But the few remaining turn of the century buildings do give us some idea of the opulence of the era.

Today, the barely 100 year old Ku'damm is still no doubt Germany's most magnificent promenade, where Berliners from all walks of life get together to see and to be seen. It has however lost its onetime elite quality (Europe's largest coffee house), or better said: the Ku'damm has gotten more democratic. Its critics have even called it "Broken Down Boulevard". As a matter of fact, the street has been heavily criticized for the way many traditional old shops have had to move into the side streets to make way for the only establishments that can afford the outlandish rents. Which is why today we find the more interesting shops, more original eateries and more atmosphere in general on the side streets than on the boulevard itself. Even so, the Ku'damm still has more than its share of first-class addresses: a number of the best hotels, restaurants and cafés, haute couture boutiques, and antique shops remain, along with a few theatres, such as the *Schaubühne* [5], which found a new home in the reconstructed Mendelsohn building on *Lehniner Platz.* With the "Skulpturenboulevard" (Sculpture Boulevard), the Ku'damm has been transformed into a controversial open air gallery.

At the corner of *Joachimstaler Strasse,* the focal point of the *Kranzler-Ecke* (Kranzler Corner) is the Café Kranzler, which achieved its international renown at its previous location on the corner of Friedrichstrasse and Unter den Linden in the East. Diagonally across the street the *Ku'damm Eck* shopping mall, complete with a wax museum, provides a healthy contrast to the Europa Center. The third mall, the *Ku'damm-Karree,* is situated between the Ku'damm and Uhlandstrasse. At Fasanenstrasse 24, the new *Käthe-Kollwitz-Museum* was opened in 1986, with drawings, sculpture and graphics by Käthe Kollwitz (1867–1945). Between Fasanenstrasse und Uhlandstrasse you will find an atmospheric shopping arcade with exclusive stores and restaurants.

Individuals with time to put two and two together should catch a look at the *new math clock* at the intersection of the Kurfürstendamm and Uhlandstrasse – the illuminated sign tells the time: the upper line showing five hours a square, the next one one hour, the third five minutes and the bottom row the individual minutes.

Walk 2: Bahnhof Zoo – Ernst-Reuter-Platz – Tiergarten

The point of the departure for this walking tour is again the *Bahnhof Zoo*. From here we turn into *Hardenbergstrasse*, this time in a northwesterly direction. Directly to your right you will find the *Bundesverwaltungsgericht* (Federal Court House). In front of this, *Jebenstrasse* runs down the side of the railroad station. At No. 2, you will find the:

Kunstbibliothek Berlin [6]

(Hours – see p. 23)

(Hours – see p. 23)

The Art Library of the Prussian Cultural Heritage Museums contains 180,000 volumes dealing with all aspects of the fine arts. It is made up of the *Lipperheid Costume Library* (15,000 volumes, 40,000 illustrations of general and folk costumes), the *Graphics Collection* (hand-drawn sketches and engravings from the Gothic era to the modern day), the *Grisebach Collection* (on the history of European book printing art) and the Collection of Architectural Drawings, Commercial Art and Posters (about 100,000 sheets). Special exhibitions take place regularly.

We continue along Hardenbergstrasse to *Fasanenstrasse*. On your right, at the corner of Hardenbergstrasse and Fasanenstrasse, you will find the *Hochschule der Künste* (Academy of Arts; music, drama, fine arts, design and music education, architecture), built in 1902, with its theatre and a modern glass-enclosed annex containing the concert hall (1,360 seats). The sculpture in the foyer is "Concerto" by Hans Uhlmann. Some of Europe's most important artists are on the faculty here, and the student body numbers over 4,800 (1990). On the left hand side of the Fasanenstrasse (No. 79/80) you will find the:

Jüdisches Gemeindehaus [7]

The Jewish Community Center was built on the site of the former synagogue, destroyed by a Nazi mob in 1938. The portal of the old synagogue and a memorial column made up from the remains of the old building have been integrated into the new building. Today it is the gathering place of Berlin's Jewish community, which, with its approximately 6,500 members, a pathetic shadow of the 170,000 who lived here before the nightmare of the Hitler era, is nevertheless the largest in Germany. Some 200 Jews also live in East Berlin. One of the synagogues is nearby at *Pestalozzistrasse No. 14*.

Across the street from the Jewish Community Center you will find an extremely original flea market, the *Zille-Hof*, decorated with reproductions of the ultimate Berliner's art works. The market sells everything from used clothing and linens all the way to busts of Frederick the Great and Bismarck and is open every day except Sunday from 8:30 to 5:30.

On nearby *Steinplatz*, we find a stone memorial to the victims of Fascism. It is made of stones recovered from the conflagrated Fasanenstrasse synagogue; another memorial pays tribute to the victims of Stalinism. These are followed by the modern buildings of the Technische Universität (Technical University), running from here to *Ernst-Reuter-Platz*. Passing the Renaissance Theater (in front of it August Gaul's 1911 "Duck Fountain") and crossing the street, we come to:

Ernst-Reuter-Platz [8]

This square is truly a showplace. Its 41 fountains were placed here in the 1950's by Düttmann and Hermkes and can be seen in all their glory during the summer. The square is surrounded by modern office buildings, among them the 22-story Telefunken Building, the 9-story IBM Building, the Eternit Administration Building, and, on the *Strasse des 17. Juni* (commemorating the workers' uprising in East Berlin on that date in 1953) and *Hardenbergstrasse* the new buildings of the Technische Universität. On *Marchstrasse* you will find Bernhard Heiliger's 1963 memorial to Ernst Reuter (West Berlin's first Governing Mayor from 1950–1953 and before that Mayor of all Berlin), the 17-foot high, glowing "Flame".

Near Ernst-Reuter-Platz, on *Otto-Suhr-Allee* you will find the small *Tribüne (Tribune) Theatre* [9], and on *Bismarckstrasse* the *Schiller-Theater* [10], constructed in 1950/51 (1,067 seats; reliefs by B. Heiliger in the lobby, one of Berlin's leading dramatic theatres. Not very far away – on the other side of Bismarckstrasse – is the *Deutsche Oper Berlin* [11], built in 1961 by Fritz Bornemann. In front of the 230-foot long windowless facade, made of concrete panels inlaid with colored pebbles, is an abstract sculpture by Hans Uhlmann (1961). Modern sculptures decorate the extensive foyers.

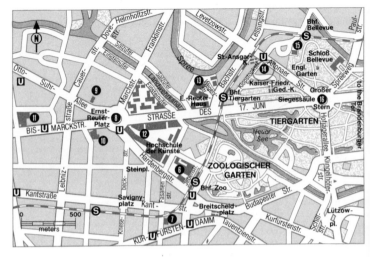

Running from Ernst-Reuter-Platz eastward is the *Strasse des 17. Juni,* which is almost two miles long – ends at the *Brandenburg Gate* (see p. 52). On its right hand side is the main building (1880) of the:

Technische Universität [12]

The Technical University (TU) was an outgrowth of the Königlich-Technische Hochschule (Royal School of Science and Engineering), which was founded in 1879, making it West Berlin's oldest institute of higher learning. Between the end of the Second World War and the present day, a number of new institutes were set up, the buildings of which run in one direction to *Fasanenstrasse* and in the other (north) up the Strasse des 17. Juni to the *Einsteinufer* (Heinrich Hertz Institute). A department of philosophy joined the TU's natural science and engineering faculties in 1950. The TU has around 32,000 students.

The street crosses the *Landwehr Canal* via the *Charlottenburg Bridge* (1907), decorated with bronze statues of King *Frederick I,* and Queen *Sophie Charlotte.* Following on the left is the Ernst Reuter House, where the Senate Library, the German Institute of Urban Studies and the Berlin Representation to the Assembly of German Cities have their homes. *Wegelystrasse* leads off westward from the *Tiergarten S-Bahn station,* to the:

Staatliche Porzellanmanufaktur [13]

The State Porcelain Factory had its beginnings here with the Berlin Porcelain Factory, established by W. C. Wegely in 1751, and purchased by Frederick the Great on behalf of the Prussian State in 1763. To this day, the blue scepter of Brandenburg is still the factory's trade mark. *The exhibition rooms on Wegelystrasse and the sales rooms at Kurfürstendamm 205 are open Mon.–Fri. from 9–6 and Sat. from 9–2.*

*Tiergarten

This magnificent nature park, about 2 miles long and a half mile wide, was once the Elector's hunting grounds and game enclosure. About 100 years ago, the renowned landscape gardner *Peter Joseph Lenné* (1789–1866) created one of Europe's loveliest parks here. Lenné's shady paths, little lakes and streams, crossed by small bridges, give the park its individual touch to this day. During and immediately following the war, the Tiergarten was totally laid waste, stripped of its trees and turned into farm land. With the planting of the first linden tree by Mayor Ernst Reuter at the "Grosser Stern" (Great Star) in 1949, reforestation began. Since then, over a million young trees and shrubs have been planted here, and today, the Tiergarten, with its 20 miles of paths, is once again Berlin's ultimate beauty spot. Favorite stopping points inside the park are the *New Lake* (rowboats, café), the *Rose Garden,* and the *English Garden,* donated by Great Britain's Queen Elizabeth II and officially opened by her then Foreign Minister, Sir Anthony Eden, later the Earl of Avon. Most of the numerous monuments, some of them placed in fairly concealed locations, date back to around 1900.

At the northern edge of the Tiergarten a unique example of urban renewal, the:

*Hansaviertel [14]

No other Berlin district was as horribly ravaged by the Second World War as the Hansa District, situated between the *Tiergarten* and *Bellevue* S-Bahn stations. It had to be completely evacuated. In the framework of the "International Architectural Exhibition 1957", 48 noted architects from 13 countries (among them *Walter Gropius, Alvar Aalto, Oscar Niemeyer* and many others) designed this prime example of what an inspired housing project can look like. Many different types of building, ranging from one-family dwellings to skyscrapers, were put up here. In addition, we find two churches, representing the two major Christian denominations – the Protestant *Kaiser - Friedrich - Gedächtniskirche* (Emperor Frederick Memorial Church) and the Roman Catholic *St.-Ansgar-Kirche* (St. Ansgar's Church), its bells donated by Konrad Adenauer – as well as a school, a library, shops, restaurants, an internationally known children's theatre called the *Gripstheater*, and the district's own subway station (Hansaplatz). You will find a plaque on each building bearing the name of its architect. Even today, the Hansa district can be regarded as exemplary urban living at its highest level.

Akademie der Künste [15]

The construction of the Academy of Arts was made possible by a gift from German-American philanthropist Henry H. Reichhold and constructed on Hanseatenweg in 1960 according to plans by Berlin architect Werner Düttmann. Since then, the academy has developed into one of Berlin's most important cultural centers. One of its watchwords is: "acquainting the public with the artistic trends of our time". Its exhibitions are always of the very highest rank; the intention is not merely to present individual objects but rather display coherent entireties.

The academy is made up of the exhibition building, the studio building with its theatre auditorium and a building with ateliers, guest and conference rooms. The academy was established in 1954 in the tradition of the Prussian Academy of the Arts, which, founded by Frederick III in 1696, was the third oldest art academy in Europe (after Rome and Paris). In its present form it encompasses the areas of architecture, art, music, literature and dramatic art. Outside the main entrance, you will find Henry Moore's large "Reclining Figure" (1956).

After our visit to the Hansa District, we continue on down *Altonaer Strasse,* past the *English Garden* to the *Grosser Stern* (Great Star), an expansive circular public square, about half way down the *Strasse des 17. Juni.* In the middle we find the:

Siegessäule [16]

Observation platform open Tues. – Sun., 9–6, Mon., 3–6 – closed in winter.

The Victory Column was built on the former "Königsplatz" (Royal Square) in 1873, and was designed by Heinrich Strack to commemorate the Prussian wars with Denmark (1864), Austria (1866) and France (1870/71). The monument, enlarged from 200 to 223 feet when it was repositioned, consists of a granite pedestal, a round substructure supported by 16 columns (with a *glass mosaic* designed by Anton von Werner depicting Germany's 19th century wars of liberation and unification), and the main column, made of sandstone and decorated with the gold-plated, 27-foot tall, 1,500 lb. victory goddess *Victoria* (by Drake). From the 164-foot high observation platform, you have a magnificent *view of Berlin.

Victory Column

Walk 3: Siegessäule – *Brandenburger Tor – *Nationalgalerie

From the Großer Stern (Great Star), the *Spreeweg* leads to:

Schloss Bellevue [17]

Bellevue Palace Gardens are open (when the Federal President is not in residence).

Bellevue Palace was built in 1785 by Daniel Philipp Boumann for Prince Ferdinand, Frederick the Great's youngest brother. The interior was designed by Carl Gotthard Langhans. Up until the First World War, it served as residence for a number of Hohenzollern princes. Badly damaged in World War II, it was totally renovated, starting in 1954, to be used as the *Federal President's official residence in Berlin*. Among the rooms reconstructed was Langhans' classic-style oval ballroom.

Walking along the banks of the Spree, we come to a building, part of which collapsed in 1980, the:

Kongresshalle [18]

The Convention Hall was put up in only 15 months as the United States' contribution to the "Interbau '57", made possible by funds from the Benjamin Franklin Foundation, and called the most daring building in all of Europe (the bold design was the work of American architect Hugh A. Stubbins). It owes its nickname "the pregnant oyster" to its vaulted roof construction, which bears some resemblance to an open oyster. The damaged building was reopened in 1987.

John-Foster-Dulles-Allee leads to the *Platz der Republik*. The west side of the square, today totally empty, was once the site of the Kroll Opera House, where Otto Klemperer and his eminent associates once made operatic history with their daring, innovative productions of old and new works in the 1920's. In later years, after a great portion of Germany's most important artists had been forced out of the country, the building was taken over for the meetings of Hitler's rubber-stamp parliament, following the Reichstag fire. It was torn down in 1951.

Between the Convention Hall and the Reichstag Building is the new *Carillon*, which, with its 68 bells, is the fourth largest in the world. It plays twice daily for five minutes (12 noon and 6 p.m.). Directly at the spot where the Berlin Wall once stood we find the:

Reichstagsgebäude [19]

The Reichstag Building was erected between 1884–1894 by Paul Wallot, in a style based on the architecture of the Italian High Renaissance. In 1933 the building was partially destroyed by arson, then totally demolished in the allied air attacks in 1945. In the years 1957–1971 the Reichstag was reconstructed (without the large dome however). On October 4, 1990 – after fifty-seven years – a freely elected German Parliament assembled here in the reunited Berlin. There is a permanent exhibition of German history and other changing exhibitions. Restaurant. *The Reichstag is open daily, except Mon. 10–5.*

To the South of the Platz der Republik, fronting on the Strasse des 17. Juni, is one of this divided city's peculiarities, the *Sowjetisches Ehrenmal* (Soviet Monument) [20]. The monument, built in the shape of a wide gate of honor, was put up in 1946 and is guarded day and night by Soviet soldiers.

From the Platz der Republik, you can continue on to *Brandenburg Gate*, which was made into a pedestrian crossing point shortly before Christmas 1989.

If you go south from the Reichstag along Entlastungsstrasse (Bellevuestrasse branches off from this street and leads to the still dreary *Potsdamer Platz,* once the busiest square in Europe; from here Leipziger Strasse leads to Mitte), you will reach Kemperplatz, where on the southern edge of the Tiergarten surrounding the Late Classic *Matthäuskirche* (St. Matthew's Church; built in 1846; restored in 1958), a new museum and cultural center has come into being ("Kulturforum").

*Philharmonie [21]

The Philharmonic Hall, home base of the world-renowned Berlin Philharmonic Orchestra, was constructed by Hans Scharoun between 1960–1963. The octagonal, ochre building with its sweeping roof is one of the boldest designs in the history of modern architecture and was the cause of storms of controversy. The 200-foot long, 18-foot wide and 68-foot high concert hall (capacity: 2,200) is also distinguished by its excellent acoustics. In May 1988 the *Kammermusiksaal* (Chamber Music Hall) based on plans by Sharoun, was opened in the Philharmonic Hall (capacity: 1,000).

The Philharmonic Hall is flanked by the newly built *Musikinstrumentenmuseum* (Musical Instruments; 1984) and the *Kunstgewerbemuseum (Museum of Applied Arts; 1985)*. The latter offers an overview of applied arts in Europe from the Early Middle Ages (the **Treasure of the Guelphs is world famous, as are many of the Carolingian and Romanesque church treasures) through the Renaissance (*Lüneburg Municipal Silver Collection, Italian and Spanish majolica), the Baroque era (glasses, faiences), the turn of the century (art nouveau) up to the present day.

Staatsbibliothek [22]

The State Library in Potsdamer Strasse was also designed by Hans Scharoun and was constructed between 1967 and 1978. It contains some 4,000,000 books covering all areas of scholarship, as well as manuscripts, autographs, bequests, music, special collections, the Mendelssohn Archive, inter alia; the library also subscribes to about 30,800 different periodicals. Concert hall.

*Nationalgalerie [23]

The newly constructed National Gallery, designed by Ludwig Mies van der Rohe, was opened in 1968. It contains works of art removed from the old National Gallery and stored in the West when the war ended, as well as the "Gallery of the 20th Century", which makes it one of the most impressive collections of 19th and 20th century works in the world. Well-represented are German and French Impressionists and German Expressionists. The principal stress of the Surrealism collection is laid on the works of *Max Ernst, Francis Bacon, Lam* and *Mattá*. Young contemporary artists are also well represented, e.g. the Germans *Penck* and *Kiefer*. Sculptors worth mentioning here include *Barlach, Maillol, Rodin, Schadow, Scheibe* and *Moore*.

About 5 minutes walk from the National Gallery, at *Stauffenbergstrasse 13/14* we find the courtyard of the one-time military Supreme Command Headquarters ("Bendler Block") and the *Memorial to the Victims of July 20, 1944* [24]. The monument, designed by Richard Scheibe and put here in 1953, commemorates the unsuccessful plot of military officers Beck, Olbricht, Count von Stauffenberg, Mertz von Quirnheim and von Haeften to assassinate Hitler. The conspirators were executed by firing squad here in the night of July 20, 1944. Exhibition.

Nearby, on the Landwehr Canal, we find the new *Bauhaus Archive Building* [25], one of Walter Gropius' late works. Gropius had chosen the city of his birth to have this plan realized.

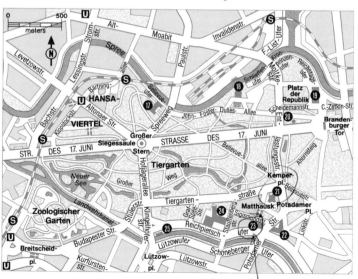

National Galerie

31.

On *Luisenplatz,* opposite the old mile post (about 1800) which bears the inscription "1 mile from Berlin" (that is to say about 4 miles from Dönhoffplatz, Berlin's geographic center at the time) – is Schloss Charlottenburg (Charlottenburg Palace). Across the street, flanking *Schloss-Strasse* on the left and right the palatial twin barracks, which today house the Museum of Antiquities (western building, see p. 33) and the Egyptian Museum (eastern building, see p. 33). They were built between 1851 and 1859 by Friedrich August Stüler, a pupil of Schinkel's.

*Schloss Charlottenburg [26]

Charlottenburg Palace, the largest and handsomest palace in the city, had its origins in the form of a small chalet built by architect Arnold Nering between 1695 and 1699 on orders from Electress and first Prussian Queen, Sophie Charlotte. Swedish-born architect Eosander von Göthe enlarged the palace considerably in the years between 1701 and 1712. It was he who created the high central dome over the main building and the orangerie on the west side – another one was planned for the east side, but could not then be realized. This planned east wing, the "new wing", was one of the first projects undertaken by Frederick the Great on his accession to the throne in 1740. The construction was carried out by Georg Wenzeslaus von Knobelsdorff on commission from the new king. Under Frederick William II, Carl Gotthard Langhans then built the palace theatre and the "Belvedere" tea house in the park from 1788 to 1790. After its destruction in 1943, the exterior was reconstructed in the original style. The palace today is the site of the Governing Mayor's official receptions.

Andreas Schlüter's **Equestrian Figure of the Great Elector* (1967) was placed in the palace's memorial courtyard in 1952. Its original site had been the "Long Bridge" (today's City Hall Bridge) near the Berlin town palace. Schlüter's work is the most splendid of its kind produced during the German Baroque.

The palace's *Historical Rooms* have been faithfully reproduced and are open to the public (*visiting hours: Tues. – Sun., 10 A.M.–5 P.M., Thurs. until 8 P.M.*). The rooms on the ground floor of the Nering-Eosander section are only accessible on special guided tours. Here, adjoining an enfilade, we find the *Frederick I*

Bust of Queen Nefertiti

and *Sophie Charlotte Rooms,* decorated, in the taste of the period, primarily with Chinese furniture. In several rooms, pictures by the great French portraitist Antoine Pesne hang on the walls. Frederick I had brought him to the Prussian court after 1710. The *Porcelain Cabinet* is also a much admired part of the castle, an elegantly appointed room in which a vast collection of porcelain, most of it Chinese, is on display.

The loveliest rooms in Knobelsdorff's "new wing" are on the upper floor: the luxurious *private quarters of Frederick the Great,* with *paintings by the king's favorite French artist, Antoine Watteau, alongside works of Lancret and Pater, today the largest collection of these artists' works outside of France. The *White Hall,* the king's private dining room, has also been restored, as has the *Golden Hall,* Knobelsdorff's grand ballroom, one of the most magnificent ballrooms of the German Rococo period. Up to 1985 the ground floor was taken up almost entirely with the Kunstgewerbemuseum (Museum of Applied Arts).

Founded in 1867, this was once the largest and richest of its kind in Germany. Despite heavy losses toward the end of the war, many of its sections – such as the one showing Italian majolica – still offer visitors a more unified overview than they will find in any other German museum. In 1986 this museum removed to the new building in the Tiergarten (see p. 31). Its place in the palace has been taken by the *Romantic Gallery* (Works by *Caspar David Friedrich, *Menzel, Schinkel* et al.).

In the Langhans building, the former palace theatre, we find the:

Museum für Vor- und Frühgeschichte

The Museum of Prehistory and Early History suffered extremely heavy losses in the Second World War (among them Heinrich Schliemann's important finds from Troy). The collection ranges from the stone age to the bronze age to the early and late iron ages in Europe and the ancient Orient, as well as finds from excavations in Berlin.

In the palace gardens we find the *Belvedere Tea House,* built by Langhans for Frederick William II in 1788 and now home of the *Porcelain Collection,* and the *Mausoleum* of Queen *Louise* and King *Frederick William III,* where Emperor *William I* and Empress *Augusta* also have their final resting places. The latter was built in 1810–1812 by Heinrich Gentz, based on plans by Schinkel. In addition there is the *Schinkel Pavillion* (1824/25; later restored), which drew its inspiration from a Neapolitan villa. In 1970 it was converted to a museum containing furniture (some of it actually designed by Schinkel), sculptures, arts and crafts and paintings of the period, among them some rare paintings by *Schinkel.*

In addition to the Prehistory and Early History museum section, the Charlottenburg museum section also houses two more important collections from the Prussian Cultural Heritage Foundation: the Antikenmuseum and the Ägyptisches Museum, located in the two Stüler buildings.

*Antikenmuseum

Like all of Berlin's other state museums, the Museum of Antiquities still reflects the special situation of the once-divided city: the exhibition consists exclusively of items evacuated to the western part of Germany during the war – most of them smaller pieces. The larger antique sculptures can be seen in the Pergamon Museum (see p. 57).

The prime display and most valuable possession in the museum is its *collection of Greek vases,* considered one of the most important in the world. In addition, it owns some of the most beautiful small antique bronzes from Greece and Etruria. A singularly important collection can be found in the treasure room in the basement, comprising the rich *collection of

ancient gold craftsmanship (comparable to the one in the Louvre), the *Hildesheim silver find* and the magnificent specimens of *Egyptian mummy portraits,* of which Berlin has an extensive collection.

*Ägyptisches Museum

The Egyptian Museum in Charlottenburg also displays items which had been removed to the west from the Egyptian Museum on East Berlin's museum island – primarily small sculptures. The art and artefacts from the Nile Valley on display here range from the years 4500 B.C. to the time of the Roman Empire. The greatest treasure is the 19-inch high **limestone bust of Queen Nefertiti* (ca. 1350 B.C.) found in 1912 near Tell el-Amarna. In addition there is the *Ebony Head of Queen Teje* (ca. 1370 B.C.), the **Green Head,* one of the major late period (600–330 B.C.) Egyptian sculptures, and the **Kalabsha Gate,* a gift from the late President Anwar el-Sadat.

Situated next to the Museum of Antiquities is the *Bröhan Museum* (see also p. 23), displaying collections from Jugendstil to Art Deco (paintings, drawings, sculptures, glass and ceramics). The *Gipsformerei der staatlichen Museen* (State Museum Plaster Casting Workshop) is located nearby (Sophie-Charlottenstrasse 17/18). Here you can buy copies of well-known sculptures of all eras from museums in Germany and elsewhere.

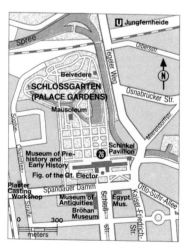

33

Walk 5: Theodor-Heuss-Platz – Messegelände – *Olympiastadion – Spandau

This "walk" covers a lot of territory, and unless you are a hardy walker, you would do better to do this route either by car or on BVG buses. The point of departure is *Theodor-Heuss-Platz*, a major traffic intersection. In the middle we see a sacrificial bowl with a flame – originally lit by Professor Heuss, West Germany's first Federal President – which was to continue burning until the reunification of Germany. On the south side of the square, we find the television broadcasting center of *Sender Freies Berlin* (Radio Free Berlin) and the *Haus des Rundfunks* (Broadcasting House; 1931) on *Masurenallee*. To the south of Masurenallee begins the expanse of the:

Ausstellungs- und Messegelände

The Exhibition Site and Fair Grounds contain 24 large, interconnected exhibition halls. The indoor exhibition area measures 807,000 square feet with an additional outdoor area of 430,000 square feet. This is the site of a number of important specialized trade fairs, such as "Green Week", a food and agricultural fair held annually in January/February, the "International Tourism Market" (February/March) and the "International Fashion Fair" (October). In the center of the halls, we find the oval summer garden with the "Palace at the Broadcasting Tower", an elegant terrace restaurant. A bridge provides a direct connection from the exhibition grounds to the *International Congress Center* (ICC), opened in 1979, on the east side of the Messedamm. A total of 80 halls are available here for conventions, congresses and cultural events, such as ballet performances, concerts, shows, etc. Outside the ICC, one of the largest congress centers on earth, there is a highly controversial giant sculpture by French artist Jean Ipousteguy. Towering over the exhibition grounds is the 450-foot tall (excluding antenna)

Funkturm [27]

The steel structured Broadcasting Tower was built in 1924–1926 for the "3rd German Broadcasting Exhibition", and is one of Berlin's most prominent landmarks. At the 180 foot level is the Broadcasting Tower Restaurant. From the observation platform (413 ft.; open 10 A.M. to 11.30 P.M.; elevator) we have a mag-

Exhibition Grounds with Broadcasting Tower

nificent *view. At the foot of the Broadcasting Tower (entrance Messedamm), the *Deutsches Rundfunkmuseum* (German Broadcasting Museum) makes its home.

To the south of the exhibition grounds we find the *Deutschlandhalle* [28], built in 1935 and restored after the war. It can accommodate 10,000 people. All kinds of large-scale events take place here. To the south of the exhibition grounds we also find Berlin's once famous auto racing track, the *Avus* (Automobile Testing Track), two straight 6 mile lanes cutting across the Grunewald and ending in Nikolassee, part of Zehlendorf.

From *Theodor-Heuss-Platz* we continue down *Reichsstrasse*, turning off at *Steubenplatz* into *Olympische Strasse*, which leads to the Olympic Stadium. We, however, recommend you go down *Heerstrasse*, turning off to the right into *Sensburger Allee;* here you will find the:

Georg-Kolbe-Museum [29]

Hours – see p. 23.

This was once the home and workshop of sculptor Georg Kolbe (1877–1947; Kolbe is buried in the Heerstrasse-Trakehner Allee Cemetery). Here we find 180 bronze figures on exhibit, as well as 1,500 sketches and hand drawings, providing an excellent overview of this artist's work. In the nearby *Georg-Kolbe-Grove* are some of Kolbe's larger-than-life-size bronzes.

We now continue down *Sensburger Allee, Heilsberger Allee* to *Olympischer Platz.*

*Olympiastadion [30]

Open daily from 8 A.M. until nightfall.

The Olympic Stadium was built by Werner March (1894–1976) for the Games of the XIth Olympiad, held here in 1936. Hitler had hoped to pervert this event to prove his theory of the physical superiority of the Nordic races, which is why, when a black American track star named Jesse Owens began running away with the medals, the infuriated Führer stormed out of the stadium. Today a street near the stadium is named for Owens, who died in 1981. The main stadium is an enormous oval, 984 feet long and 754 feet wide, accommodating some 80,000 spectators. In addition there is a swimming and hockey stadium, as well as tennis courts and an equestrian arena. We walk through the "Marathon Gate" to the *Maifeld,* which holds some 500,000 spectators. The 250 foot tall bell tower on its west side was reconstructed in 1962 and given a new (4.5 metric ton) bell. The old, cracked bell stands today at the south gate. There is a superb view from the tower (elevator).

To the south of the Stadium at the *Heilsberger Triangle* is the 17-story *Corbusier House* [31], designed by French architect Le Corbusier (1887–1965) for the "International Building Exposition 1957".

From here we continue over *Heerstrasse* and *Pichelsdorfer Strasse* (Bus 94, change to the 34 or 97) to *Spandau,* Berlin's westernmost district. On our way, we pass by the British Military Cemetery behind *Scholzplatz* and then cross a bridge over the *Stössensee* (Stössen Lake). About a thousand feet beyond here, a path leads to the wooded *Pichelswerder Peninsula* (nature preserve). Shortly before getting to the *Frey Bridge,* where we cross the *Havel,* we find a path leading off to the right down to an idyllic little fishing village called *Tiefwerder,* and nicknamed "Little Venice on the Havel". Behind the bridge, to the right of the *Grimnitzsee* (Grimnitz Lake) and the left of Heerstrasse lies the little town of *Pichelsdorf,* surrounding the *Scharfe Lanke Havel Bay,* a popular site for water sports. To our right, *Pichelsdorfer Strasse* leads to Spandau's downtown area.

Spandau

Spandau is located at the point where the *Spree* and *Havel* Rivers flow together. Spandau is older than Berlin – it received its town charter as early as 1232 and was an independent municipality up until 1920. It has preserved more of its (14th century) old city than any other West Berlin district – as a matter of fact, it is the only authentic old city anywhere in Berlin. The loveliest corner here is the newly restored *Kolk* (along with the remains of the city wall).

But Spandau is also Berlin's largest industrial area, with the *Siemensstadt,* local headquarters of the giant, multi-national electrical firm, right at its heart. In the extreme northwest of Berlin lies the large *Spandau City Forest.*

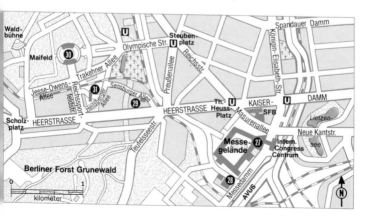

In the old city of Spandau, on *Reformationsplatz* we find the:

Nikolaikirche [32]

Built mainly in the 15th century, St. Nicholas' Church is the last preserved example of Marchic brick Gothic architecture in Berlin. In its restored *interior we take special note of the bronze *baptismal font* (1398) and the painted *limestone altar,* donated by Count Rochus von Lynar in 1582; on the north wall of the nave is a Gothic *crucifixion scene* (1540).

In front of the church is Encke's *Monument to Elector Joachim II* (1889), together with Schinkel's *War Memorial* (1816), erected to commemorate the Wars of Liberation (1813–1815). About a third of a mile north-east of this, on the left bank of the Havel, we find the:

Spandauer Zitadelle [33]

The moated Spandau Citadel was started in 1560 according to plans drawn by Italian architect de Gandino, based on the new fortress system introduced in Italy at the time, with sharp-cornered bastions; de Gandino designed the gatehouse and the "King" and "Queen" bastions. Starting in 1578, work was continued under the direction of Count Rochus von Lynar, who built the "Crown Prince" and "Brandenburg" bastions. The mighty walls surround, among other things, the remains of Spandau Fortress (ca. 1520) and the 105 foot high *Julius Tower* from the middle of the 13th century, the same time when the *Palas* was constructed. This residence and public hall building, adjoining the Julius Tower, is the most elegant structure in the fortress. The large

Spandau Citadel

Gothic hall inside was reconstructed in 1981. The Julius Tower served for a while as a prison. After the Franco-Prussian War of 1870/71, the golden treasures given by France to Prussia as war reparations were stored here. Since 1962, the citadel has been studied by archaeologists and restored. – *City History Museum* and castle restaurant.

Also part of Spandau are two former fishing villages on the Havel, *Gatow* and *Kladow,* both popular excursion sites. The *Kladower Damm* leads from Gatow to Kladow, today a fancy suburb. On *Imchenallee,* which runs down the banks of the Havel, we find a number of charming garden inns as well as a boat dock and a number of swimming areas. Just off the coast is the little *Imchen Island* (bird sanctuary). A walk over the *Ritterfelddamm* to the *Gross-Glienicke* district on the banks of *Gross-Glienicke Lake* is also highly recommended. The G.D.R. frontier ran right through the middle of the lake.

Drivers may choose to return to town along the former city limits route: from Kladow in a northwesterly direction over the *Ritterfelddamm,* past the British military airfield in *Gatow* to the former *Ritterfeld Estate* and from there to the right down the *Potsdamer Chaussee.* The adjoining *Wilhelmstrasse* in Spandau was the location of the Allied Military Prison, where Nazis convicted of war crimes at the 1946 Nuremberg trials were incarcerated. After the death in 1987 of its last inmate, Hitler's one-time deputy Rudolf Hess, the prison was demolished. Shortly before this street, *Heerstrasse* on your right will get you back into town.

Walk 6: Through the Grunewald to the Wannsee

See map – p. 38.

You get to the Grunewald, Berlin's picturesque forest, on the U-Bahn, the bus or in your own car. Leave the downtown area via *Hardenbergstrasse, Ernst-Reuter-Platz, Bismarckstrasse, Kaiserdamm* and *Heerstrasse*. When you get to *Scholzplatz* turn left into the road *Am Postfenn*, which runs across the northern tip of the Grunewald to the Havel. The connecting *Havelchaussee* (6.6 miles) between Grosse Steinlanke and Lieper Bays is closed for cars.

The *Grunewald

The 15 square mile forest is part of the Wilmersdorf and Zehlendorf districts and begins south of *Heerstrasse*, ending some 6 miles to the south at the *Wannsee*. It is bordered on the west by the *Havelchaussee* (see following description) with its many bays and beaches. Its south and east sides contain a number of lakes, such as the *Schlachtensee* and the *Krumme Lanke* in the Nikolassee section of Zehlendorf (the best way to get to both these lakes is subway to the *Krumme Lanke Station* and then across *Argentinische Allee* and down *Fischerhüttenstrasse*).

Both lakes have several small swimming areas. A popular restaurant among the Berliners is the "Alte Fischerhütte" on the Schlachtensee (rowboat rental). It's a good idea to finish off a walk around these two lakes with a visit to the "Haus am Waldsee", which offers a variety of exhibitions, primarily of modern artists (Zehlendorf, Argentinische Allee 30).

From here it is only a few minutes by car to Zehlendorf-South and the *Museumsdorf Düppel* (Düppel Museum Village), Clauertstrasse 11, which you can also get to on Bus No. 3. A mediaeval village (ca. 1200–1220) has been reconstructed here on the Machnower Fenn. The attractions include demonstrations of building construction, pottery and weaving. Hours: Spring to Fall, Sundays 10–5. The Museum Village is at the edge of the *Düppel Forest*, which runs between the Nikolassee and Wannsee sections of Zehlendorf directly along the southwestern edge of the city, one of Berlin's four large forest areas. The Düppel Forest is Berlin's quietest forest, and even in summer it is not overrun with people. Sometimes you can walk for miles in this area without meeting a soul. You can take a long circular hike starting at the *Stahnsdorfer*

Damm, which leads off of Potsdamer Chaussee. The Grunewald suffered badly in the Second World War; 44% of its tree stock was destroyed. About 24 million trees were planted here after the war, 6 million of them leafed trees, which have given a brighter face to what was once a rather gloomy pine wood.

A few fens, moors and little lakes are under government protection – deer, boars and smaller animals all make their homes here. The *Teufelsberg* (377 ft.), near *Teufelseechaussee* by the *Teufelsee*, was created out of war rubble and then covered with topsoil and cultivated. With its toboggan run, two ski jumps with ski tows and snow cannons for artificial snow, this mountain is the city's "winter sports center". Teufelssee and Teufelsfenn have been protected sanctuaries since 1960. The area is fenced in.

The road *Am Postfenn* leads down to the *Havel*, which you can follow to the south down the *Havelchaussee*. Beyond the *Jürgenlanke Havel Bay* you can see the *Schildhorn Peninsula*. Here, on a small promontory stands a *sandstone pillar* with a shield and a cross on it, in remembrance of the flight of Jaczo, the last Prince of the Wends, from Albrecht the Bear. He and his horse got away by swimming across the Havel, and in gratitude he is said to have converted to Christianity.

The road now leads around the *Dachsberg* (200 ft.) to the *Karlsberg* (260 ft.) with its 184 foot high:

Grunewaldturm [34]

The Grunewald Tower was built in old Märkish red brick style in 1898 and originally called the *Kaiser-Wilhelm-Turm* as a memorial to Emperor William I. The observation platform, 443 feet above the Havel, affords a magnificent *panorama of West Berlin from Spandau all the way to Potsdam. The "Grunewaldturm" restaurant is also there.

The Havelchaussee returns to the Havel by the *Lieper Bay*. A little farther down the road you will find a ferry boat to the attractive island of *Lindwerder*. The road runs parallel to the shore down to the *Grosse Steinlanke Bay*, then crosses the woods, reaching *Kronprinzessinnenweg* at the southern curve of the *Avus* (see p. 34). You follow this road to *Nikolassee*. From here you can drive to *Wannsee*.

You can also turn right from Kronprinzessinnenweg down *Wannseebadweg,* which leads directly to:

Strandbad Wannsee [35]

Wannsee Beach is Berlin's largest outdoor swimming area, called the "Berlin Lido". It was opened in 1907 and expanded in 1930 by Martin Wagner and Richard Ermisch. The mile long, 260 foot wide sandy beach welcomes up to 30,000 people on sunshiny days. The view from the thatch-roofed Wannseeterrassen Restaurant just outside the swimming area is one of the nicest in town.

Wannseebadweg leads on to the island of *Schwanenwerder* – the island has been inhabited since 1882 and now has a dam connecting it to the mainland. Colorado's *Aspen Institute,* an organization promoting improved relations between top management executives on both sides of the Atlantic, as well as fostering improvements in Berlin's economic, cultural and intellectual life, has its Berlin Headquarters here. Shortly before you get to the dam, you will see a little footpath on the right leading to the *Grosses Fenster* ("Big Window"), from which you have a view across the Havel all the way to Spandau.

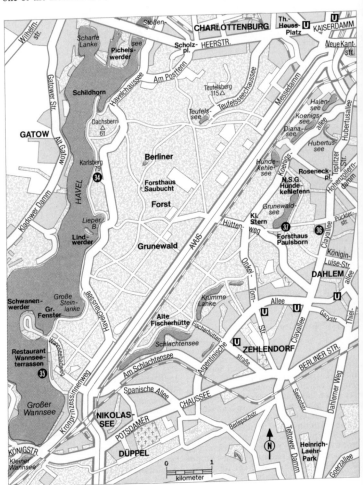

Walk 7: All Around the Grunewaldsee

We get from the *Kurfürstendamm* to the start of this excursion on Bus 19 (or 29), getting off at *Roseneck*.

From here we go along the Grunewald, down *Clayallee* (named for General Lucius D. Clay, the Military Governor of the U.S. zone of occupation in Germany, who oversaw the Berlin air lift) to *Pücklerstrasse*, or else you can take Bus 50 from Roseneck to Pücklerstrasse. If you just want to visit the Grunewald Hunting Lodge or go down to Grunewald Lake you should get off the No. 50 at *Königin-Luise-Strasse*. This road turns off to the right and leads directly to the hunting lodge and then down to the Lake.

*Brücke-Museum [36]

Bussardsteig. Hours: see p. 23.

This museum was opened in 1967 on the initiative of painter *Karl Schmidt-Rottluff*, who gave the museum a great number of his works. It is dedicated to the painters who founded the expressionistic movement called "Die Brücke" (The Bridge) in Dresden in 1905. Later the Brücke painters found a new home in Berlin. The greater part of the exhibition here is taken up with the paintings of *Schmidt-Rottluff* and *Erich Heckel*. Other Brücke artists represented here include *Ernst-Ludwig Kirchner*, *Max Pechstein*, and *Otto Mueller*, as well as artists associated with the group, such as *Max Kaus*, *Emy Röder*, *Otto Herbig* and *Emil Nolde*, who only belonged to the "Brücke" briefly.

We continue down a footpath to *Grunewald Lake*, where, directly adjoining the lake, we find the:

*Jagdschloss Grunewald [37]

Open in summer Tues.–Sun., 10–1 and 1:30–5.

The Grunewald Hunting Lodge was built in Renaissance style in 1542 by Caspar Theyss for Elector Joachim II. In 1593, architect Rochus von Lynar added the farm building and the stables. During the reign of Frederick the Great, around 1770, additional farm buildings were added. The interior decoration dates mainly from the time of King Frederick I. The lodge served as a refuge for Kings Frederick William II and William III. – The cozy rooms on the ground floor bring

Grunewald Hunting Lodge

to mind the hunting tradition of this chalet: beautiful old Baroque furniture, precious Berlin porcelain, hunting trophies, hunting and animal illustrations (17th/18th centuries). Upstairs, a remarkable collection of paintings by German and Dutch masters (15th to 19th centuries) has been assembled, including works by *Blomaert, Bruyn, Bol, Jordaens* and *Rubens*, as well as *Cranach the Elder* and *Graff*. Portraits from the Frederician period and Berlin's Biedermeier era supplement the collection. – A small *Hunting Museum* has also been set up there.

After visiting the hunting lodge you can stop in for a little refreshment either at the almost 160 year old Forsthaus Paulsborn (right) or the Chalet Suisse, to your left on the way back to *Clayallee*. Or you can go for a stroll down the banks of Grunewald Lake, this typical Markish lake, then across the adjoining *Hundekehlefenn* natural preserve in the north to the *Königsallee*, which cuts across the elegant Grunewald suburb and connects the Kurfürstendamm with the Grunewald. Going down Königsallee, we pass, on our left, *Diana Lake* and the *Königssee*, to the right *Hertha* and *Hubertus Lake*, then a *Memorial to Foreign Minister Walther Rathenau*, the only Jewish government minister during the Weimar Republic, who was murdered here (corner of Wallottstrasse) by bigoted fanatics on June 24, 1922, one of the first overt acts of the Nazi terror which would soon overwhelm the entire nation. Behind the *Halensee* is the beginning of the Kurfürstendamm, which will take you back downtown.

Walk 8: Wannsee – *Pfaueninsel – Kohlhasenbrück

This route leads to the extreme southwest tip of the city, with its glorious forest and lake scenery and cultural monuments. The quickest way to get to *Wannsee* by car is via the *Avus* (see p. 34). You can ride the S-Bahn from the *Zoo Station* to *Wannsee Station* and go from there to Pfaueninsel (Peacock Island) with Bus 66.

Across the street from the Wannsee Station, why not go into the hilltop park and get a magnificent view of the *Grosser Wannsee*, a 761 acre bay on the Havel? A chain of smaller lakes is attached to it: *Kleiner Wannsee, Pohlesee, Stölpchensee* and *Griebnitzsee*. You can get to these lakes down *Bismarckstrasse*, which leads off *Potsdamer Chaussee*. Right at the beginning of the road, a little off to the right, you'll find the *Kleistgrab* (Grave of the poet and dramatist Heinrich von Kleist 1777–1811), who ended his life on November 21, 1811, in typical *Sturm and Drang* style, in a bizarre suicide pact with a terminally ill woman named Henriette Vogel. Below the park, across the *Grosser Wannsee*, is the dock for the boat to *Kladow, Pfaueninsel* (Peacock Island), *Nikolskoe, Potsdam, Caputh, Werder*, etc.

If you want to drive to Peacock Island, turn right off *Kronprinzessinnenweg* into *Königstrasse*. Shortly before you get to *Volkspark Glienicke, Nikolskoer Weg* goes off to the right, taking you to the boat dock. No dogs are allowed on Peacock Island. No smoking.

*Pfaueninsel [38]

This natural sanctuary and popular excursion site is about a mile long and some 1,600 feet wide. The history of Peacock Island goes back to the 17th century. In 1685 the Great Elector equipped a laboratory here for an alchemist named Johann Kunckel to make gold. Instead, Kunckel succeeded in making improvements in ruby glass, a highly treasured item in those days. "Kunckel glasses" became world famous.

The *castle* (open daily, except Mondays, from April to October, 10–4) on the southwestern tip of the island was built between 1794 and 1797 by Potsdam court architect Brendel, in keeping with the taste of the period, in the form of an artistic ruin, for Countess Lichtenau, Frederick William II's mistress. The façade and the bridge connecting the two towers were

Castle on Peacock Island

originally made of wood; later this was replaced by wrought iron and concrete.

A walk around the island takes us from the castle to *Jacob's Fountain*, the *Cavalier House* (in the middle of the island; expanded by Schinkel in 1826), the *dairy farm* (at the northern end; built in 1795), to the *Queen Luise Memorial Temple* and on to the bird house and greenhouse. In essence, however, it is not so much the architectural treasures on the island that make for its charm but rather the luxuriant foliage: centuries-old oaks, mammoth California pines, Asiatic ginkgos, and a single cedar of Lebanon, presented to Emperor William II on his visit to the Near East on a fact-finding mission, prompted by the Viennese journalist Theodor Herzl. The tree was planted by the Emperor himself in 1898. In *Peacock Court* you will actually find genuine peacocks. In 1984, a brook, a waterfall and a pond were set up here in traditional style.

The dock on the mainland is also point of embarkation for another popular destination: *Nikolskoe* and the nearby Church of Sts. Peter and Paul. The *Blockhaus* (log building) in authentic Russian style was put here in 1819 by Frederick William II for his daughter, Charlotte, the future Russia Czarina. The original building burned down, but a new log house has been placed on its site, and is today one of Berlin's nicest country restaurants. The *Kirche St. Peter und Paul* (Church of Sts. Peter and Paul; 1834–1837) was also built

40

in Russian style. The carillon in the church tower plays a tune between 12 and 6 every day, but don't look for any bells up there – it's a tape recording of the carillon in the Potsdam Garrison Church, which was badly damaged and later torn down.

The road winds around *Moor Lake Bay* then turns into a footpath which passes the Klein-Glienicke Volkspark, finally reaching *Glienicke Bridge,* which now again provides a direct link between Klein-Glienicke and Potsdam. The East German border ran right through the middle of the bridge – the East Germans called it "Unity Bridge". It was regularly featured in the news as the bridge where East and West exchanged "unwanted persons". About 100 yards away from it you will find a building restored in 1984:

*Schloss Klein-Glienicke [39]

Klein-Glienicke Castle acquired its present form in 1826, when the brilliant architect Schinkel rebuilt a chalet constructed there in 1764 for Prince Karl, son of Queen Luise, turning it into an Italian-style summer residence. Worked into the walls are relics of sculptures and architectural remnants which Prince Karl brought back from a trip to Italy. The castle today houses a restaurant.

The romantic 222 acre *Volkspark Klein-Glienicke* was laid out at the beginning of the 19th century by landscape gardener Peter Joseph Lenné (1789–1866). It contains a number of remarkable buildings, such as Schinkel's 1835 *Great Curiosity*.

To the south of *Königstrasse* is the *Jagdschloss Glienicke* (Glienicke Hunting Lodge), built in 1854 but originating from a hunting lodge (1682) belonging to the Great Elector. It was converted in 1885, and the main building was again converted in 1963. Today it is a an adult education center. A bit farther on, to the south of Königstrasse in the Wannsee direction, stands the 216 ft. *Böttcherberg*.

From the hunting lodge, Königstrasse runs straight through to the Wannsee S-Bahn station. But before you leave, we suggest a little detour to the chain of lakes to the south of the Wannsee, and to:

Kohlhasenbrück

Here, in 1540, Michael Kohlhaas, a man depicted in Kleist's novel as a victim of corrupt and uncaring authorities, determined to get his revenge, is said to have robbed a coach containing silver and hidden the stolen goods. A long dead end leads down the *Teltow Canal* to *Albrechts Teerofen* (Albrechts's Tar Stove), until reunification surrounded on all sides by G.D.R. territory.

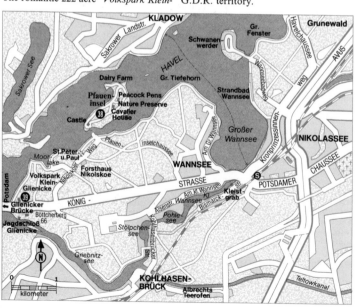

Walk 9: Freie Universität – **Museum Dahlem – *Botanischer Garten

This route begins at the U-Bahn station *Oskar-Helene-Heim* (outside the university hospital on Clayallee), then moves across the Dahlem University Campus to the nearby Botanical Gardens.

Freie Universität [40]

The Free University (FU) was founded in 1948 after the division of the city. Its first Rector was Friedrich Meinecke, a noted historian who died in 1954. Between 1950 and 1954, the *Henry Ford Building,* the university's modern main building, containing the Auditorium Maximum, and the *University Library Building* were constructed, all made possible by funds from the Ford Foundation of the United States, a foundation that has taken a special interest in Berlin's cultural life and has sponsored a number of projects in the western part of the city. A number of other new buildings followed these first two, but a substantial part of the university is still housed in former mansions on the quiet suburban Dahlem streets. And yet, for all its many buildings, the university is bursting at the seams. In 1990, the student body numbered some 58,000 (all pursuing graduate studies – Germans get their "liberal arts" education in high school) – quite a contrast to the 1,500 waiting to study here when the university opened its doors in 1948. With its Free University, Technical University and Academy of Arts, Berlin leads Munich as the city with the largest student population in Germany – around 108,000 in fact. This figure does not include the ca. 25,000 students in the eastern section of the city.

The U-Bahn takes us to Königin-Luise-Strasse. Here in Dahlem Village Square, where the timber-frame structure of the *Dahlem-Dorf U-Bahn Station* still gives us an impression of what things must have been like in the village surrounding Dahlem Estate, we find the mediaeval *St.-Annen-Kirche* (St. Anne's Church; 14th and 15th centuries). In the churchyard are the final resting places of historian *Friedrich Meinecke* (1862–1954), animal sculptor *August Gaul* (1869–1921) and a number of important actors.

**MUSEUM DAHLEM [41]

Arnimallee 23–27 and Lansstrasse 8, U-Bahn station Dahlem-Dorf and Buses nos.1, 10 and 17. For hours see p. 23.

The world-famous Berlin museums shared the fate of the divided city. Today they are concentrated primarily in four areas: Charlottenburg Palace, Dahlem and the area south of the Tiergarten District in the western part of the city as well as their one-time gathering place, Museum Island in the eastern part. When, starting in 1953, the art treasures removed for safekeeping in mines and bunkers during the war were returned to Berlin, the ones stored in East Germany were sent to East Berlin, while the items stored in West Germany landed in West Berlin. In other words they all owe their present location to coincidence. Of course, West Berlin had to create new facilities to house them. The building finally chosen was the *Asiatic Museum* in *Arnimallee.* Started in 1914 but not then completed, it was greatly expanded by a number of additions after the last war. Today, Dahlem Museum is the most important museum in the western part and contains as part of the Prussian Cultural Heritage Foundation the *Ethnological Museum,* the ***Painting Gallery,* the *Sculpture Division,* the *Copperplate Engraving Collection* and the *Museums of East Asian, Islamic* and *Indian Art.*

The main entrance for the Painting Gallery, the Sculpture Division and the Copperplate Engraving Collection is on Arnimallee.

***Gemäldegalerie

The Painting Gallery provides a magnificent overview of all periods of European painting from the 13th to the 18th century, concentrating primarily on German, Italian and Dutch painting, and is internationally important both in terms of the quality and the quantity of its art works. Although the painting collection was split up by the war and its consequences – one part here in Dahlem, the other in the painting gallery on Museum Island – new acquisitions have given each collection its own distinctive personality. It is now no longer evident that the two collections are the product of chance, even though neither of the two galleries has been able to approach the completeness the Berlin Gallery had at the turn of the century.

14th and 15th century Italian art is gloriously represented in Dahlem with masterworks by *Botticelli, Fra Filippo Lippi, Veneziano, Verrocchio, and others. One high point is **Raphael's Five Madonnas. Works by *Mantegna, Bellini, Giorgione, as well as Titian ("Venus with the Organ Player", "Self Portrait") represent upper Italian painting, while the 18th century Venetian School is primarily represented by Tiepolo and Canaletto, many of whose *Venetian scenes are on display. The Italian collection in Dahlem is doubtless the most significant collection of its kind outside Italy.

And the Dutch section is every bit as important. With 21 **Rembrandts, among them the world-renowned ***"Man with the Golden Helmet" (possibly not authentic), *"Hendrickje Stoffels", two self-portraits and portraits of Rembrandt's wife Saskia, the gallery owns one of the largest Rembrandt collections in the world. In addition there are famous paintings by Jan van Eyck, *Pieter Brueghel ("The Dutch Proverbs"), Hugo van der Goes, Frans Hals (**"Malle Babbe"), Terborch (*"The Concert"), Vermeer van Delft (**"Lady with a Pearl Necklace") and a large number of Rubens'.

The German division includes masterpieces by Albrecht Dürer ("Portrait of Hieronymus Holzschuher", 1526), Albrecht Altdorfer (*"Calm on the Flight", "Nativity"), Martin Schongauer (**"Adoration of the Shepherds") and Lucas Cranach the Elder (**"Fountain of Youth"). Another highly admired work is Hans Holbein the Younger's **"Portrait of the Merchant Georg Gisze".

A number of 17th and 18th century French masters, including Nicolas Poussin, Claude Lorrain, **Watteau ("French Comedy", "Italian Comedy"), Pesne, and

"Man with the Golden Helmet"

others are on display. El Greco (***"Mater Dolorosa"), Goya, Velazquez and many others represent the Spanish school.

**Kupferstichkabinett

The Berlin Copperplate Engraving Collection is far and away the richest of all German graphic collections, and, after Vienna, Paris and London, one of the most important in the world. Its collection of hand drawings, especially the Dutch and German masters (a vast collection of *Rembrandt and Dürer sketches, as well as pieces by Holbein the Younger, Grünewald, Altdorfer, Cranach, etc.), comprises some 23,000 items. The Berlin Rembrandt collection is the largest in the world. 27 of *Botticelli's 85 world-famous illustrations for Dante Alighieri's "Divine Comedy" are here (58 are on Museum Island). And the Venetian school of the 15th, 16th, and 17th centuries is also handsomely represented. Several of the most important of Claude Lorrain's sketches

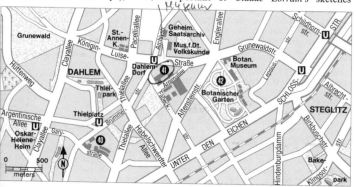

can be found here, although the greater portion of them is on Museum Island. This is also the case with **Antoine Watteau,* the important French painter and illustrator, several of whose finest works are owned by the Dahlem Museum. The high points of this collection also include German impressionist *(Liebermann, Corinth, Slevogt)* and expressionist etchings, in particular works by the "Brücke" group (see also p. 39). And then there is a handsome pop art collection. The originals will be shown on request in the study.

*Skulpturenabteilung

The new sculpture museum in Dahlem was opened in 1966. Its collection includes sculptures from late antiquity to the 19th century. The first floor has the late Antiquity collection on display, Byzantine art and its successors as well as Early and Late Mediaeval European art. One particular feature of these first two collections is a splendid collection of small pieces in ivory. When you get to the Late Mediaeval works, make certain you see the work of Franconian master *Tilman Riemenschneider* (*"Münnerstadt Evangelists", "Angel Concert") and the famous *"Dangolsheim Madonna", sculpted by a Strasbourg master (ca. 1470), as well as works of the great Lower Bavarian master *Hans Leinberger,* represented here with large and small pieces (one particularly moving piece is *"Christ in Agony").

Southern European Renaissance sculpture (15th to 17th centuries) is also extremely well represented here – we'd like to mention the "Mary of the Annunciation" (1411) by *Jacopo della Quercia,* the famous *"Pazzi Madonna", an early *Donatello,* then *Verrocchio's* *"Sleeping Youth" and *Leonardo da Vinci's* *"Flora Bust". The Northern European Renaissance is represented, inter alia, by monumental sculptures by *Martin Zürn* and works by *Peter Vischer the Younger.*

Museum für Indische Kunst

The Museum of Indian Art was founded in 1963 and contains the most important collection of Indian art in Germany. It displays bronzes, carvings, paintings and fabrics from India, Pakistan and the bordering countries. Special attractions are the *Turfan Collection* (named for the Turfan Oasis in Eastern Turkistan) with unique frescoes (ca. 500 to 900 A.D.), depicting the life of Buddha, and the *Gandhara Collection,* with Buddhist stone reliefs and sculptures (1st century A. D.).

Museum für Islamische Kunst

The Museum of Islamic Art stresses the particular importance of Arabic calligraphy in the Islamic religion. In addition, the museum displays architectural elements such as a prayer niche with two calligraphic friezes (16th century Persia), giving us some idea of Islamic architecture. Besides these items there are steles, carpets, court and religious textiles.

Museum für Ostasiatische Kunst

The Museum of East Asian Art displays the art of *China, Mongolia, Korea* and *Japan* from 1700 B.C. to the present day (bronzes, paintings, ceramics, applied arts).

*Museum für Völkerkunde

The Ethnological Museum is one of the leading museums of its kind in Europe.

It includes collections from *Africa* (impressive bronzes from *Benin* and West African masks), the *South Seas* (Hawaii, Polynesia, Micronesia, the Atoll culture) and the *Americas* (South American forest Indians, Peru, Ecuador, Chile, Northwest Argentina, Mexico, the Mayan country) as well as *South Asia* and *East Asia.*

Nearby, at *Im Winkel 6,* is the *Museum für Deutsche Volkskunde* (German Ethnological Museum), displaying furniture, equipment, folk costumes, textiles, etc., from the Germany of the 17th to 19th centuries (hours: see p. 23).

Archivstrasse 12 is the address of the *Geheimes Staatsarchiv,* the former "Secret Prussian State Archives", a historical museum containing documents from Prussia's eastern provinces, a library, a collection of family documents, and so on.

On *Königin-Luise-Strasse,* going toward Steglitz, you will find one of the entrances (the other is on *Unter den Eichen*) to the:

*Botanischer Garten [42]

Open weekdays 9–7, in Winter 9–4. Admission charge.

In the charming 104 acre Botanical Gardens the *Victoria-Regia-House* and the *Palm House* deserve our special attention. A great portion of the garden is taken up with the *Geographic-Horticultural Division,* showing flora from the mountain ranges of the Pyrenees to the Alps, Carpathians, Balkans and the Caucasus all the way to the Himalayas. Beside the entrance on Königin-Luise-Platz stands the *Botanical Museum.*

Walk 10: Schöneberg – Tempelhof – Neukölln

This route takes us through the southeastern sections of the western part of the city. We take the subway from the *Zoo Station* to the *Kurfürstenstrasse Station* in:

SCHÖNEBERG

The subway station is right in the middle of *Potsdamer Strasse.* To the north, Potsdamer Strasse leads directly to the *National Gallery, Philharmonic Hall* and *Potsdamer Platz* (see p. 30); this marks the border between this district and *Tiergarten.* To the south, the street goes through downtown Schöneberg and, with its extensions, *Hauptstrasse* and *Rheinstrasse,* takes us through the *Friedenau* section of Schöneberg, still a fairly peaceful neighborhood with quite a lot of turn of the century architecture.

In the southern part of Schöneberg, on its border with *Steglitz,* atop the *Insulaner,* a 250 foot high rubble mountain, we find the *Wilhelm Foerster Observatory* (astronomical presentations and telescope viewings Tues. and Thurs.–Sat. 8 P.M., Sun. 3, 4, 5, 6 and 8 P.M.).

Following Potsdamer Strasse south from the subway station, we find, on the right hand side of the street:

Kleistpark [43]

Kleist Park, once a part of the Great Elector's kitchen garden, turned into a public park in 1679, was for a long time the main section of the Botanical Gardens, which were then moved to Dahlem in 1900.

In the back of the park is the former *Kammergericht* (Supreme Court of Justice), where later on the Nazis held show trials, most of them presided over by the infamous judge Roland Freisler, who actually went so far as to take secret movies of himself making a mockery of every imaginable rule of law. Between 1945 and 1948, this was the meeting place of the Allied Control Council. In 1948, the foreign ministers' conference took place here, and the Four Power Agreement was signed here in 1971. On December 11, 1989, the allies came together again for the first time in 18 years, to discuss recent events in Berlin. This historic structure may be used later in an official capital city capacity or once again to house the Supreme Court. Turning from Potsdamer Strasse into *Grunewaldstrasse,* we go down *Martin-Luther-Strasse* to *John-F.-Kennedy-Platz.*

Schöneberg City Hall

Schöneberger Rathaus [44]

The Schöneberg City Hall was put up between 1911 and 1914 and is today the official headquarters of Berlin's governing mayor and the seat of the city's house of representatives. Every day at noon, in the 213 foot high tower, the *Freedom Bell* is sounded. The bell was presented to the Berliners by General Clay in 1950 and bears an inscription paraphrasing Abraham Lincoln's "Gettysburg Address": "That this world, under God, shall have a new birth of freedom." A bronze plaque by the door reminds us that at this place, on June 26, 1963, President John F. Kennedy stirred the world with his "Ich bin ein Berliner!" speech.

On the edge of *Rudolph-Wilde-Park,* to the south of here, at *Kufsteiner Strasse 69* we find the building which houses *RIAS* (Radio in the American Sector), a German-language radio and television station broad-casting to Berlin and environs under the sponsorship of the United States government.

From Schöneberg City Hall, we continue down *Dominicusstrasse, Hauptstrasse, Kolonnenstrasse* and *Dudenstrasse* (Bus No. 4) to the district of:

TEMPELHOF

Dudenstrasse ends at the *Platz der Luftbrücke* (Airlift Square), behind it the expanse of Tempelhof airfield.

In front of the one-time airport building, we find Eduard Ludwig's 65-foot high *Airlift Memorial,* which has stood here

10

since 1951. The three westwardly pointing arches symbolize the allied Airlift missions which kept the city alive during the Soviet Union's Berlin blockade in 1948/49, a series of events that proved to the Russians that Harry S. Truman was not a man to be messed with.

Zentralflughafen Tempelhof

The Tempelhof Central Airfield takes up the greater part of the *Tempelhof Field,* a parade ground during the city's imperial period. In 1908, the *Wright Brothers* demonstated their first engine-powered aircraft here. This was also the place where German civil aviation began, in 1923. In 1926, Lufthansa was founded. The present airfield building was built between 1934 and 1939. In 1975, Tempelhof closed its doors to civilian air traffic and now serves as a U.S. military air base. Civilian flights use Tegel Airport, though recently some have been handled at Tempelhof.

In the *Mariendorf* district we find West Berlin's only *trotting track* (Mariendorfer Damm). At the corner of *Mariendorfer Damm* and *Alt Mariendorf* stands the Mediaeval *Mariendorf Village Church,* a fieldstone building from the 13th century. Berlin's oldest village church (1220), the *Marienfelde Village Church,* is on the *Marienfelde* district's main square. From the Platz der Luftbrücke, *Columbiadamm* and *Flughafenstrasse* lead on to:

NEUKÖLLN

Between Columbiadamm and Hasenheide lies the *Volkspark Hasenheide,* once the Great Elector's hunting grounds. This was also the scene of a quiet revolution. In the early part of the 19th century, sports and exercise were considered unseemly and slightly immoral. A teacher named Friedrich Ludwig Jahn, citing Juvenal's maxim of "A healthy mind in a healthy body", contended that not only were athletics clean activities, they were also useful for the achievement of Prussia's political goals. A monument reminds us that the Hasenheide was the first public athletic field in the world (1811).

Flughafenstrasse leads further to the *Neukölln City Hall* (1908) on *Karl-Marx-Strasse*. The remains of a *Bohemian Village* can be found between *Richardstrasse* and *Kirchgasse*. This village was once a colony of religiously oppressed Bohemians, who, in 1737, found a new home here in Rixdorf (Neukölln's name until 1912). Today, the old blue collar district of Neukölln is where many Turkish citizens make their home – it has the largest foreign contingent in West Berlin.

The Federal Horticultural Show in 1985 turned a garden colony in the southern part of Neukölln into *Buga Park,* now called *Britzer Garten* (222 acres, 14 miles of paths, lakeside restaurant), with a number of special attractions.

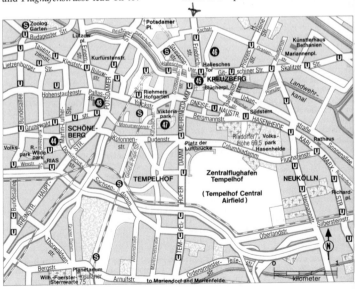

See map p. 46.

Kreuzberg is Berlin's second smallest but most densely populated district. The population, made up primarily of laborers, students and foreigners, lives here cheek-by-jowl, most of them in austere apartment buildings dating back to the turn of the century, with that Berlin trademark, the "Hinterhof", a paved courtyard. Every fourth resident here comes from another country, most of them from Turkey. Most visitors do not find a large foreign colony in a major city particularly unusual or alarming, but the Germans have had to get used to it, and friction between the local and migrant worker communities has often been harsh.

Many of the old buildings are now being restored to their former dignity (the elegant stucco façades on the *Planufer* along the Landwehr Canal are an excellent example). Another successful restoration is the *Riehmers Hofgarten* residential complex (1881–1892), a real Garden of Eden compared to some of the stark apartment houses surrounding it (Entrances: Yorckstrasse, Grossbeerenstrasse and Hagelberger Strasse). The facades on *Chamissoplatz* have also been restored.

Nevertheless, Kreuzberg is a wide-awake district, with a special charm all of its own with individualistic taverns and streets full of life. Unfortunately there are almost no green areas here.

Kreuzberg plays a very important part in Berlin's artistic life, and a number of vital impulses have come forth from here in recent years, especially from the local subculture. The "Künstlerhaus Bethanien" (a cultural center in the former Bethanien Hospital building: theatrical performances, concerts and art exhibitions) on *Mariannenplatz* has consolidated its good reputation. The *Martin Gropius Building* (Stresemannstrasse 110) has become a gallery of international rank and houses the *Berlin Gallery,* the *Jewish Section,* among other things. The building is located on the former site of the SS and Gestapo headquarters. In the vaults of the now demolished Gestapo HQ you can view the documentary exhibition "Topography of Terror". All that remains of the former *Anhalter Bahnhof* on Askanischer Platz is the restored monumental portal. The old station grounds are now used for exhibitions. The *Deutschlandhaus* (Stresemannstrasse 90) concentrates on the culture of Germany's former eastern provinces.

The best way to get to Kreuzberg from the *Zoo Station* is on the subway (Line 1), getting off at *Hallesches Tor.* The subway station is on *Mehringplatz,* which, together with Blücherplatz directly to the south, forms the center of the district. The streets leading north from here all ended at the Wall and are virtually abandoned, including *Friedrichstrasse* with "Checkpoint Charlie", the former border crossing to East Berlin for non-Germans. At *Blücherplatz* we find the: see map page 46

Amerika-Gedenkbibliothek [45]

The America Commemorative Library, Berlin's largest public library (almost 1 million volumes, immense Berlin section, modeled along the lines of a free public library in the United States), was made possible by contributions from the United States. To the south of the library are the *Cemeteries at the Hallesches Tor,* the final resting place of poets *Adelbert von Chamisso* (died 1838) and *E.T.A. Hoffmann* (died 1822), as well as of composer *Felix Mendelssohn-Bartholdy* (died 1847). Not far from here, on *Lindenstrasse,* in a handsome restored Baroque building that once housed a court of law, we find the:

*Berlin Museum [46]

In a building worthy of its subject, this museum tells the story of the city from the days of the Great Elector up to the 20th century. Main exhibitions are a portrait gallery of prominent Berliners, the Chodowiecki collection, views of the city, furniture, documents on Berlin humor, Judaica and a toy collection. Another point of attraction is the excellent "Weissbierstube", a historical tavern.

From *Blücherplatz,* the *Mehringdamm* leads southward to the *Platz der Luftbrücke.* Before you get there, turn into *Kreuzbergstrasse* and continue on to the:

Kreuzberg [47]

This 217 foot high hill (Kreuzberg means "Mountain of the Cross") gave the district its name. Crowning the summit is a *Monument to the Wars of Liberation,* built by Schinkel in 1821. The 32 acre *Victoria Park* is laid out on the mountain's slopes, complete with a waterfall and an artificial rock gorge.

11

Walk 12: Through the Wedding and Reinickendorf Districts

See map p. 49.

This is a visit to the former French sector, formed by the two districts of *Wedding* and *Reinickendorf.* The most interesting sight here is *Tegel Lake,* with its *Tegel Humboldt Castle* and *Tegel Forest.* The quickest way to get there is on the No. 9 U-Bahn line (Rathaus Steglitz – Zoo – Osloer Strasse), which connects with the No. 6 subway (Alt-Mariendorf – Tegel) at Leopoldplatz.

Drivers go from *Ernst-Reuter-Platz* (see p. 27) down *Marchstrasse* and *Franklin-strasse* (named for Benjamin Franklin) toward the northeast. This will take you to the *Moabit* section of the Tiergarten District, a place a few local citizens would be happy to avoid – the criminal courts and houses of detention are located here. Behind the *Spree,* you turn left, then immediately to the right into *Beusselstrasse,* at the end of which a bridge over the Westhafen Canal leads right up to the *Plötzensee Juvenile Detention Home,* where over 3,000 victims of Nazi terror, including the conspirators in the Hitler assassination plot, were executed. In the prison courtyard we find the *Gedenkstätte Plötzensee* (Plötzensee Memorial) to the victims of the Third Reich.

Heckerdamm continues on from here to the Church of:

*Maria Regina Martyrum [48]

Another memorial to the victims of the Nazis, the Church of St. Mary Queen of Martyrs was built between 1961 and 1962 by Würzburg architects Hans Schädel and Friedrich Ebert. The building was financed by contributions from Germany's Roman Catholic community. Adjacent to the church are the parish house and the large *Ceremonial Courtyard* with its *Open-air Altar,* a powerful bronze block, its pedestal encircled with a crown of thorns. On the church's right lateral wall we find the *Stations of the Cross,* which – like the altar – are the work of architect Otto Herbert Hajek. Seven different sized abstract groupings serve to summarize the fourteen stations of the cross.

In the *Lower Church,* beside the altar, we find three tombs, the one on the left the symbolic tomb of *Cathedral Provost Bernhard Lichtenberg;* the one on the right contains the remains of *Dr. Erich*

St. Mary Queen of Martyrs

Klausener and the one between them is a symbolic grave for all the martyrs denied a proper burial, or whose burial place is unknown. – The tower of Maria Regina Martyrum was originally supposed to be 157 feet high, but air safety laws (the airport isn't very far away) will not allow any structures in this part of town to be any taller than 80 feet.

We turn around, start back, go down *See-strasse,* and find ourselves in

WEDDING

Wedding is a tradition-rich blue collar district, full of nondescript apartment houses with their inevitable back court-yards, plus the factories and offices of international corporations (AEG, Osram, Schering, etc.). In the 1920's, this was the favorite gathering place of the city's Communists (especially around Kösliner Strasse). Very little of the character of old Wedding has been preserved to this day. Most of the historical parts of town have been subject to some pretty mindless "urban renewal", meaning the buildings have been torn down, including many an old structure well worth preserving, places that might have served to document the history of this district. As in Kreuzberg, the streets near where the wall once was are still quite empty of life and reflect the monotony of a ghost town. A particularly heartbreaking example of this is *Bernauer Strasse* in the southeast, where the buildings on the G.D.R. side were emptied and then leveled to their ground floors. Since the unification this depressing situation has been somewhat ameliorated.

48

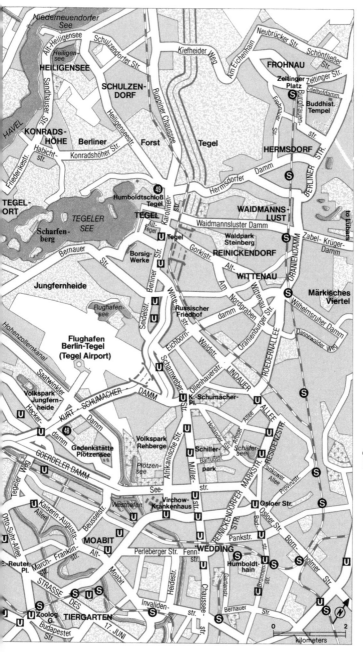

One famous "Weddinger" was the painter *Otto Nagel*, whose left-wing leanings caused him to be prohibited from painting during the Nazi era. He wound up in a concentration camp. This proletarian artist's pictures are today on exhibit in the Otto Nagel House in the eastern part of Berlin (see p. 59).

Our path goes down *Seestrasse*, past Berlin's large hospital, *Rudolf-Virchow-Krankenhaus*, to *Müllerstrasse*, where we turn left. It takes us to the district of:

REINICKENDORF

After *Kurt-Schumacher-Platz*, Müllerstrasse turns into *Scharnweberstrasse* then *Seidelstrasse* (going past Tegel Airport and Tegel Penitentiary), finally becoming *Berliner Strasse*, as it goes past the *Borsig Plant* to the *Tegel U-Bahn Station*. From there it is only a few minutes down a street called *Alt-Tegel* to the beautiful 2 mile long *Tegel Lake*, with its beach promenade, restaurants and large bathing beach. The 1,000 acre lake is a perfect spot for all kinds of water sports.

*Humboldt-Schloss Tegel [49]

Adelheidallee 19–20. Open Sun. 2–6, closed in winter.

The "Little Humboldt Castle" started life as a country chalet during the reign of Joachim II (around 1550). Between 1821 and 1824 it was rebuilt by Schinkel for Wilhelm von Humboldt. Today it is still the property of the Humboldt family descendants. The two-story building is flanked by towers at the four corners decorated with Christian Daniel Rauch's reliefs depicting the gods of the eight winds and based on the "Tower of the Winds" in Athens.

The interior, also designed by Schinkel, is full of memorabilia of the two brothers, *Wilhelm von Humboldt*, the philologist who founded the University of Berlin, and *Alexander von Humboldt*, explorer and scientist: furniture, ancient sculptures (some of them now displayed in copies) and family portraits.

In the beautiful, expansive *Castle Gardens*, a linden arcade passes by the 400 year old Humboldt Oak to the *Humboldt Family Tomb*, designed in 1830 by Schinkel and completed in 1831 with the erection of a copy of Thorwaldsen's "Hope".

After viewing the castle, you should definitely take a stroll in the evocative,

almost forgotten *Russian Cemetery* (Wittestrasse 37). The Brotherhood of St. Vladimir bought the property from a Wittenau farmer in 1890. In 1893 the cemetery was opened, and not only were the trees planted here brought from Russia; so was the earth in which they stand. In 1894, the beautiful (restored) *Sts. Constantine and Helena Chapel* was built. Under the Cyrillic lettering of the gravestones many from Czarist Russian refugees have found their final resting places. Among them is the one-time Minister of War and General Adjutant of the Czar, *Vladimir A. Sukhomlinov*, who died a Russian exile in Berlin in 1926. The handsomest memorial here is the one dedicated to Russian court conductor and renowned composer *Mikhail Glinka* (1804–1857), who died in Berlin but was buried in his homeland.

Starting at the castle, *Karolinenstrasse* and its extension Ruppiner Chaussee wind their way over the hilly landscape of the Tegel Forest to *Schulzendorf* and the former village of *Heiligensee* (directly on the former city border). To the south, on the peninsula between the Havel and Tegel Lake are the popular summer excursion sites of *Konradshöhe* and *Tegelort*.

Going as far as the northernmost border district in the city is well worth the time and trouble. You can get there from the Tegel Station with BVG buses: take line 15 to *Hermsdorf* and *Frohnau*, and No. 20 to *Waidmannslust* and *Lübars*.

Hermsdorf, founded as far back as the 13th century, has developed into a lovely country home colony.

Frohnau, set up here around 1900 by Prince Henckel von Donnersmarck as a garden colony, has one of the few *Buddhist Temples* in Europe (Edelhofdamm 54). The building was constructed in East Asian style between 1922 and 1924 for physician and philologist Dr. Paul Dahlke. Since 1963 its owner has been the "Buddhist Society of Sri Lanka", which sends monks here to serve the congregation.

And, last but not least, let us recommend a visit to the more than 700 year old farm village of *Lübars*, to the north of the controversial "Märkisches Viertel" housing project. On the village square we find the little church, built in 1793, old farms and a jolly tavern, "Zum lustigen Finken". Lübars is the only village in Berlin where the farmers actually still concentrate their attentions on farming the land.

Walk 13: *Brandenburger Tor – *Unter den Linden – Dom

The Brandenburger Tor (Brandenburg Gate) can be reached by walking down the Strasse des 17. Juni, by car via Potsdamer Platz/Leipziger Strasse or by driving past the Reichstag via Scheidemannstrasse and Clara-Zetkin-Strasse.

*Brandenburger Tor [50]

The first, rather unimpressive, gate was put up here in 1734, one of a total of 18 gates in the city wall.

After Prussia had become a major European power under Frederick the Great, his successor, Frederick William II, commissioned the construction of a worthy terminating point for Unter den Linden, the city's new grand boulevard. Modeling his work on the Propylaea, the great entrance hall to the Acropolis in Athens, the great architect Carl Gotthard Langhans created his masterwork with the new Brandenburg Gate, constructed between 1788 and 1791, a structure that also represented one of the most significant achievements of German Classicism. The sculptured decorations and the completion of the *Quadriga* with the goddess of victory took until 1794. The Quadriga and the goddess Victoria were the work of Gottfried Schadow. The large Attica relief represents the *Triumphal Procession of the Victory Goddess,* the 32 metopes on the front scenes from Greek mythology, the 20 bas reliefs on the walls depict the *Labors of Hercules,* and the two statues in the niches on the north and south side the goddess *Athena* and the god *Ares.* The main structure of the gate is 215 feet wide, 36 feet deep and 85 feet tall. The central passageway is 18½ feet wide, the four side passageways each 12¾ feet.

In 1806, Napoleon abducted the Quadriga as a symbol of his triumph, but Marshall Blücher brought it back to Berlin in 1814 following the wars of independence. In the 19th and 20th centuries, the Brandenburg Gate was the scene of a number of huge military parades and triumphal marches, of splendid receptions and revolutionary events (1848 and 1918). The Gate was badly damaged and the Quadriga totally destroyed in World War II.

Between 1956–1958, East Berlin had the

Brandenburg Gate

Gate restored: the Quadriga and Victoria were recast from the intact original forms in West Berlin and returned to their positions facing the other way. Shortly before Christmas 1989, before a host of political dignitaries from East and West, the Gate, since the building of the Wall in 1961 such a poignant symbol of the divided city, was opened as a pedestrian crossing point, an event celebrated euphorically.

Pariser Platz

All the buildings on this square – originally constructed on commission from Frederick William I – were destroyed in World War II. These included the French and American Embassies, the legendary Adlon Hotel (setting of Vicki Baum's novel "Grand Hotel" on which the motion picture of the same name, starring Greta Garbo, Joan Crawford and the Barrymore brothers, was based), and the home of painter Max Liebermann, who, after looking out his window at the torchlight procession celebrating the Nazi party's election victory on January 30, 1933, closed the curtains on the Linden side of his house and never opened them again. Today the new buildings of the former G.D.R. ministries and some embassies are located on the square itself and the adjacent section of Unter den Linden. Nearby, at *Schadowstrasse 10,* is the sculptor *J. G. Schadow's* home. The French Cultural Center is located at *Unter den Linden 37.*

*Unter den Linden

The ¾ mile long (from the Brandenburg Gate to Marx-Engels-Platz), 200

13

foot wide grand boulevard with its quadruple column of linden trees was originally laid out in the middle of the 17th century on orders from the Great Elector. It was given its present-day form in the reign of Frederick the Great. In World War II it was badly hit. The historical buildings in the Linden Forum were rebuilt during the 1970's, with a goodly number of new buildings added in the western section.

Friedrichstrasse leads south to *Leipziger Strasse*, then down to the international border crossing. The Komische Oper is on *Behrenstrasse*, which runs parallel to Unter den Linden. On the north side of the "Linden", Friedrichstrasse takes us to *Friedrichstrasse S- and U-Bahn station*, not far from the *Theater am Schiffbauerdamm, where Bertolt Brecht's Berliner Ensemble still makes its home.*

On Friedrichstrasse itself are the new *Friedrichstadtpalast Variety Theatre* and the *Metropole Theatre*. If we go down Unter den Linden toward Marx-Engels-Platz, we see on the left hand side of the street the *German State Library,* located in the neo-Baroque structure which was formerly called the Prussian State Library.

Humboldt-Universität [51]

The main building of the present Humboldt University was constructed between 1748 and 1766 by Johann Boumann as a palace for Prince Henry, the brother of Frederick II. In 1810, on the initiative of the renowned philologist Wilhelm von Humboldt, it was turned into an institute of higher learning (Frederick William University) and in 1949 it was renamed Humboldt University. Its first Rector was the great philosopher Johann Gottlieb Fichte (1762–1814). Other world-renowned scholars on the faculty here included the philosophers Hegel and Schleiermacher, the philologists Jacob and Wilhelm Grimm (whose "Fairy Tales" were actually a scholarly collection of stories gathered for a comprehensive study of the German language), the physicists Hermann Helmholtz, Max Planck, Albert Einstein, Max von Laue, Lise Meitner, the chemist Otto Hahn, the physicians Rudolf Virchow, Robert Koch and Ferdinand Sauerbruch, to name but a very few.

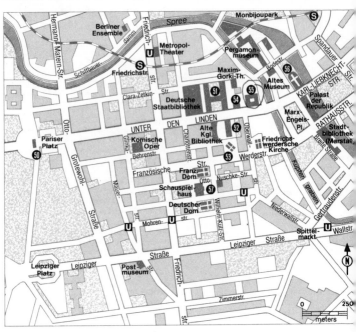

In front of the university, Christian D. Rauch's *Equestrian Statue of Friedrich II* (1851) has been returned to its place of dominance in the middle of the road.

Across the street, we find the *Women's Federation Building* (1891), beside it a new building with the Baroque facade of the *Former Governor's House* (1721), followed by William I's palace, called the *Old Palace* today. It was built between 1834 and 1836 by Langhans the Younger; its façade has been restored.

Across from the university is the beginning of *Bebelplatz,* the *Forum Fredericianum,* originally planned by Frederick the Great, which, along with the *Opera House,* the *Old Library,* and *St. Hedwig's Cathedral* goes together to make up a magnificent urban composition.

Deutsche Staatsoper [52]

The German State Opera was built between 1741 and 1743 under Frederick the Great by G. W. von Knobelsdorff as the Royal Opera. In 1843 it burned down to its foundations, but was rebuilt in its original style. Again in World War II it was totally destroyed. After a historically authentic reconstruction in the years 1952 to 1955 (only the auditorium – seating 1,452 – was partially redesigned), the theatre was reopened in 1955 and underwent a complex restoration process in 1986. Today it is the home of one of the finest opera companies in the world.

St.-Hedwigs-Kathedrale [53]

St. Hedwig's Cathedral was begun in 1747 on orders from Frederick the Great with plans by Jean Legeay and completed in 1773 by Boumann, with the Roman Pantheon as a model. It was badly damaged in World War II and reconstructed from 1952–1963. Today it is the cathedral church of the Roman Catholic Bishop of Berlin. Organ recitals: Wed. 3:30 P.M.

The *Old Royal Library* was built by Boumann between 1775 and 1780 on the west side of Bebelplatz. Almost totally destroyed in World War II, it was reconstructed between 1965 and 1969.

The former *Princesses' Palace* (1733–1811) to the left of the opera was also restored. It now houses the Opera Café.

*Neue Wache [54]

The New Guardhouse was built by Karl Friedrich Schinkel from 1816 to 1818 based on a Roman fort and once served to house the King's Guard. After the removal of the war damage it was rededicated in 1960 as the "Memorial to the Victims of Fascism and Militarism". Today there are plans to provide the New Guardhouse with a broader function: to commemorate the victims of all wars and tyrannies.

Behind the New Watch is the classicist *Singakademie Building* (1827), built here on the suggestion of Carl Friedrich Zelter, a friend of Goethe's. Today it is the home of the Maxim Gorki Theatre.

*Zeughaus [55]

The Armory is Berlin's largest Baroque building and one of the most beautiful in Germany. It was built between 1695 and 1706 by Grünberg, Schlüter and Jean de Bodt, based on original plans by Nering. Schlüter was largely responsible for the sculptures and also created the **22 *Masks of Dying Warriors* in the interior courtyard (Schlüterhof). This building too was badly damaged in the war and authentically reconstructed.

From 1952 until September 1990, it was the home of the *Museum für Deutsche Geschichte* (Museum of German History), which was closed because it presented history exclusively from the perspective of the Socialist Unity Party. It will house exhibits for the Deutsches Historisches Museum (German Historical Museum) until the new museum building designed by Aldo Rossi is completed.

Across the street from the Armory, at the site where the Command Post (1802) once stood, we now find the former *Foreign Ministry* (1967). The monument to the eminent diplomat Baron *Stein* has been restored to its former place in front of the building. At the *Werderscher Markt* we find Schinkel's Neogothic brick *Friedrichswerder Church* (1824–1828) – converted into the Schinkel Museum in 1987. We cross *Marx-Engels Bridge,* which was originally called Castle Bridge when Schinkel built it (1822–1824, restored 1982–1984). The restored statues on the bridge were also Schinkel's creations. We now continue over a Spree Canal called *Kupfergraben* and arrive at

Marx-Engels-Platz

This was once the pleasure garden (set up as a kitchen garden in 1573) and the grounds of the Berlin City Palace, which was demolished in 1951. From 1451 to 1918 it was the residence of the Hohenzollerns, and when it was torn down, protests could be heard from both East and West, because this castle was one of the most important Baroque architectural monu-

13

ments in Germany, a building on which Schlüter had worked from 1698 to 1706, followed by Eosander von Göthe, who completed his contribution in 1813. The *Eosander Portal* was incorporated into the main façade of the former *Parliament Building*, a complex which came into being between 1962 and 1964.

To the left, at the corner of Breite Strasse, rises the one-time *military stable* (see p. 59), and to the right of the former Parliament Building beyond the Kupfergraben on the Werderscher Markt, the *Headquarters of the Socialist Unity Party Central Committee*, which was disbanded after the "gentle revolution" in 1989. In 1976 the *Palace of the Republic* was opened beside the Spree on the site of the blown-up city palace. The Palace had to be closed before the end of the G.D.R. due to dangerously high levels of asbestos.

Dom [56]

Berlin Cathedral was constructed by Julius Raschdorff in the style of the High Italian Renaissance between 1894 and 1905. The exterior renovation of the cathedral, which was badly damaged in the Second World War, was completed in 1984.

Inside, work is also progressing, and the restored "Imperial Staircase" was opened on June 30, 1989. Underneath the church is the *Hohenzollern Crypt*, where *The Great Elector, King Frederick I*, and *Frederick William II* are buried.

Walk 14: *Brandenburger Tor – Platz der Akademie

Instead of taking the previously described route from the Brandenburg Gate down Unter den Linden to the cathedral, we suggest you take a little detour through the former *Government Quarter* and across the one-time *Gendarme Market* back to the *Linden*. This part of the downtown area – first laid out by King Frederick I as *Friedrichstadt*, with its two main axes, *Leipziger Strasse* and *Friedrichstrasse* – was very badly damaged in the Second World War.

Shortly after passing the Brandenburg Gate, you turn right into *Otto-Grotewohl-Strasse*, a street that bears the imprint of history. Up until the outbreak of the Second World War, the British Embassy, the Presidential Palace, the Foreign Office and the Chancellery as well as a number of ministries were all situated here. On *Leipziger Strasse*, once one of the busiest shopping streets in Berlin, Ernst Sagebiel's former Aviation Ministry (1934–1936) has remained more or less intact. Until 1990 it was the headquarters of a number of *G.D.R. ministries*. Turning left into Leipziger Strasse, we arrive at the *Postal Museum*, on the corner of *Mauerstrasse* in the former Royal Postal Ministry building. Now, turning left into Friedrichstrasse, we continue via *Mohrenstrasse* to the:

Platz der Akademie [57]

Up until 1950, this square was known as the Gendarme Market, after the "Gens d'Armes" regiment, which had its guardhouse and stables here between 1736 and 1782. In 1950 the square was rechristened in conjunction with the 250th anniversary of the Academy of Sciences. The academy's presidium is located on Otto Nuschke Strasse. On the west side of the square is the *Schauspielhaus*, once a famous dramatic theatre and one of Schinkel's most beautiful buildings (1819–1821). He built it on the foundations of the National Theatre (constructed by Langhans the Elder in 1802), which had burned down in 1817. After restoration, the badly war-damaged building was reopened in 1985 as a concert hall. The *Schiller Monument* by Begas (1868) on the square in front of it was replaced here in 1988.

On each side of the Schauspielhaus stands a cathedral: the *German Cathedral* on the south and the *French Cathedral* on the north, both of which were built shortly after 1700, with domed towers added by Gontard between 1780 and 1785. The French Cathedral was built for the French Huguenot congregation who had settled in Berlin from 1685 to avoid religious persecution in France. To this day, the community continues to hold its services here. The small *Huguenot Museum* tells the stories of the Huguenots first in France and then later in Berlin and Brandenburg (Fontane Documents). The French Cathedral has been restored. Work has begun on refurbishing the dome figures on the German Cathedral. The dome was replaced in 1984. On the corner of Charlottenstrasse and Mohrenstrasse the 600-bed "Domhotel" was completed at the end of 1990.

Walk 15: **Museumsinsel

Despite the division of Berlin's art treasures occasioned by the division of the city (see pp. 33 and 42), **Museum Island** remains one of the most important museum complexes in the world. The museum center dates back to a decree issued by Frederick William III stipulating that the art works owned privately by the Royal Family should be henceforth made accessible to the general public, for which purpose a public museum was to be created such as the ones already in existence in London and Paris.

The first to be opened was Schinkel's *Old Museum* (1830), one of his most magnificent creations, and after Munich's Glyptothek, the second oldest museum building in Germany. As it proved too small to house all the treasures, the *New Museum* (1843–1859) was soon added behind it (designed by Stüler); this building was destroyed, but is now being reconstructed in the original style, an almost Sisyphean task after the building had been allowed to fall into ruins completely in the decades after the war. The Egyptian collections are to be housed here later. In 1876, the *National Gallery* was opened, and in 1904 Ernst von Ihne's *Kaiser-Friedrich-Museum* (1897–1903), the present *Bode-Museum*. The last museum to be placed here was the *Pergamon Museum,* started in 1909 and, because of the confusion of the First World War, not completed until 1930. In October 1990 an official memorandum on the spatial and structural reorganization of the Berlin State Museums was presented. According to this plan there are to be three separate centers: the collections of antiquities are to be assembled on Museum Island, Occidental collections at Kemperplatz and ethnology at Dahlem. This reorganization would reflect the "historical reality", i.e. the different direction in which the museums have gone during the decades of division.

Except for the *Museum of Applied Arts* in Köpenick Castle, all the divisions of the East Berlin State Museums are unified here on Museum Island.

*Altes Museum

The badly war-damaged Old Museum was reopened after reconstruction in 1960 and displays works from the *New Division of the 20th Century* from the National Gallery – around 40,000 sketches, water colors, etc., among them more than 6,000 *pieces by *Adolph von Menzel* and 5,000 *Karl Friedrich Schinkel sketches* – as well as a *copperplate engraving collection,* containing around 130,000 items from the 15th century to the present day, with important pieces by *Botticelli* (for Dante's "Divina Commedia", the remainder of the exhibition is in West Berlin's Dahlem Museum), *Grünewald,* *Claude Lorrain* and *Watteau.* – The "New Berlin Gallery" displays a changing collection of contemporary art from all over the world.

*Nationalgalerie

The National Gallery was constructed by Johann Heinrich Strack from 1867 to 1876, based on plans by August Stüler, in the form of a Corinthian temple. Over the years the gallery suffered horrible losses, and not just during the war. Even before the bombs fell, the Nazis initiated a crusade to root out allegedly "degenerate art", which cost the museum some of its best works. Other significant collections are now in the western section. Yet, for all this decimation, the museum still provides an excellent overview of the development of art (painting and sculpture) in Germany from the end of the 18th century to the present day. Well represented are the works of such Berlin artists as *Krüger, Blechen, Menzel* (including the famous "Iron Rolling Mill"), *Liebermann, Ury,* then paintings by *Slevogt* and *Corinth,* masterpieces by *Caspar David Friedrich* and *Arnold Böcklin* ("Isle of the Dead"). German impressionists here include *Kirchner, Pechstein, Nolde, Rohlfs* and

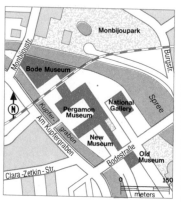

Pergamon Altar

others. There are sculptures by *Barlach* and *Lehmbruck* and 19th century works by *Schadow* ("Princess Group", "Goethe Portrait"), *Canova, Rauch* and *Begas.* The French impressionists are also gathered here. The National Gallery also owns the world famous "Maypole" by the brilliant Spanish court painter *Francisco de Goya* (1736–1828). From the 20th century, the Bauhaus, Brücke and Blauer Reiter movements are represented, and there is a collection of photomontages by John Heartfield.

***PERGAMON-MUSEUM

The Pegamon-Museum is far and away the best known museum on Museum Island. This large, three-winged building was built between 1909 and 1930 from plans by Alfred Messel (1853–1909). It contains the **Antiquity Collection* with the world-famous ***Pergamon Altar (access to altar steps at 11 A.M. and 3 P.M. only), the **Near Eastern Museum,* the *Islamic Museum,* the *East Asiatic Collection* and the *Ethnological Museum.*

**Vorderasiatisches Museum

The museum offers a comprehensive overview of 4,000 years of Near Eastern history, art and culture. Its wealth is comparable only to that in the British Museum in London. Its particular area of distinction is the vast collection of architectural monuments, of which the ***Processional Road from Babylon* and Nebuchadnezzar II's **Ishtar Gate* (604–562 B.C.) are probably the best known (rooms 8 and 9). The road is shown here with a width of only 28 feet,

when in fact it was really 53 feet wide. On each of the walls of the road we see one row of relief yellow lions on a blue background. Across from the Ishtar Gate stands the large *Court Façade of the Parthian Palace of Assur* (1st millennium B.C.).

And another unique exhibition is the *Fortress Gate of Senjirli* (10th to 8th century B.C.), flanked by four lions, the *Victory Stele of the Assyrian King Asarhaddon* (680–669 B.C.), the *Relief Tiles* and the *Giant Bird of Tell Halaf* (ca. 900 B.C.).

**Antikensammlung

The history of the Collection of Antiquities goes back to the time of the Great Elector. It was not, however, until the reign of Frederick the Great that the collection gained in importance, with acquisitions such as the purchase of Cardinal de Polignac's collection from Paris, 1742 (especially the Roman portraits), the purchase of the famous "Praying Boy" (4th century B.C.) and the inheritance of the Bayreuth Margravian collection (1758).

But the most prized possession here is the ***Pergamon Altar* (180–160 B.C.) in the central hall, the ultimate masterwork of Hellenic architecture. Tiles of the giant frieze were worked into the west side of the altar, the remaining friezes hang on the walls. These 395-foot long friezes show the battle of the gods versus the giants. Above the monumental altar staircase you come into the room with the *Small Pergamon Frieze,* the "Telephos Frieze"; in the center of the room is a *Floor Mosaic from the Palace of Attalos II* (160–150 B.C.). Another showpiece is the ornate, two-storied **Market Gate of Miletus* (ca. 165 A.D.) from the time of Emperor Marcus Aurelius.

Among the superb works of early Greek sculpture, one piece well worth mentioning is the *Goddess with the Pomegranate* (ca. 575 B.C.), the so-called Berlin goddess, which is distinguished by the remarkable way in which its colors have been preserved. In addition there is the *Enthroned Goddess of Tarento* (ca. 470 B.C.) and the bronze statue of the *Praying Boy* (end of the 4th century B.C.), all works of international significance.

Islamisches Museum

Museum director Wilhelm von Bode was responsible for the establishment of the special Islamic division in 1904. The collection offers a comprehensive overview of Islamic art from its beginnings to the present. The central object in the collection is the *Ornate Façade of the Desert Castle of Mshatta* (ca. 740 A.D.), a gift from the Turkish Sultan Abdulhamid to Emperor William II. The *Aleppo Room* (1600–1603), taken from the home of a Christian merchant, has been rebuilt here in its original form. The vast *Collection of Persian and Indian Miniatures* (14th–18th centuries) and the *Monuments of the Pre-Islamic Sassanid Dynasty* (excavated in Ctesiphon) are also well worth a visit.

Ostasiatische Sammlung

The central point of the East Asian collection, established in 1907 by Wilhelm von Bode and badly decimated during the war, is the collection of *Chinese Art*, especially the ceramic collection with pieces from the Neolithic era to the modern day.

Museum für Volkskunde

The Ethnological Museum lost around 80 % of its stock during the Second World War and had to be built up virtually from scratch. Changing exhibits.

*BODE-MUSEUM

This museum opened its doors in 1904 as the Kaiser-Friedrich-Museum and was then renamed in 1956 for its founder, Wilhelm von Bode (1845–1929), who, in his many years as General Director of Berlin's Museums, established the reputation of the city's museums at home and abroad. Besides the *Prehistoric and Early Historical Museum* (only special exhibitions), the building houses the following museums and collections.

*Ägyptisches Museum

The Egyptian Museum offers an overview of Egyptian culture from the prehistoric and early historic period (around 5000 to 2778 B.C.) to the Greco-Roman era. The museum was founded in 1820 with the purchase of a number of important collections, to which finds from the large-scale excavations of the German Orient Society were then added. Even though the museum has yet to go into its new quarters, an amazing amount of material is now on display, including objects of international significance.

The most important of these items are *King Narmer's Alabaster Baboon* (ca. 3000 B.C.), the *Reliefs from King Ne-us-er-Re's Temple to the Sun and from the Death Temple of Sahure*, the *Cubed Hassock of Sen-Mut* (ca. 1500 B.C.), the *Stuc-*

co *Head of Ikhnaton* and the unfinished *Head of Nefertiti* (her painted limestone bust is in Charlottenburg, see p. 32). A rich collection of coffins, mummies and mummy portraits and since May 1989 the spectacular "Golden Treasure" from the pyramid of a Mesoitic queen give us an excellent idea of burial practices in Ancient Egypt.

The *Papyrus Collection*, with its 15,000 or so papyri, Ostraka (potsherds) for short notes) and parchments, is one of the largest in the world. Documents and letters in Greek give us a considerable insight into everyday life in those days.

Frühchristlich-byzantinische Sammlung

The Early Christian-Byzantine Collection comprises primarily Mediterranean art from the 3rd to the 18th century. There is an excellent display of art of the Egyptian Christians (Copts); the showpiece of the Early Byzantine epoch (3rd to 9th century) is the *Apse Mosaic from the Church of San Michele in Africisco in Ravenna* (545). Considerable space has been devoted to the excellent collection of late Byzantine ikons from the Mediterranean area and Eastern Europe.

Skulpturensammlung and Gemälde-galerie

Although over half of the previous stock is now in Dahlem (see p. 42), the Sculpture Collection and Painting Gallery still houses many important works, in particular Italian Renaissance sculpture (e.g. *Donatello, della Robbia, Andrea Guardi*). The most important German sculpture here is from the 15th and 16th centuries: *The Naumburg Crucifix, *The Trier Prophets, *The Minden Altar*, and works by *Riemenschneider*. The exhibition in the painting gallery stresses the works of 17th century Dutch and Flemish masters (*Jan Brueghel the Elder, Jordaens, Ruysdael, Bol, Terborch*, etc.), followed by the Italian division (15th to 18th century): *Lippi, Reni, Canaletto, Tiepolo*, etc. The English school is represented by *Gainsborough* and *Raeburn*, the French by *Poussin* and *Pesne*, the German by *Graff*.

Münzkabinett

The Numismatic Collection is not only the oldest part of the museum, but also one of the largest and most impressive of its kind in the world, with some half a million coins, medallions, bank notes and seal stamps from all periods from the beginnings of the art of coinage to the present day (only accessible by appointment).

Walk 16: Altstadt – Alexanderplatz – Karl-Marx-Allee

This walk will take us through the oldest parts of the city, the districts of *Cölln* (on the northern half of today's Museum Island) and *Berlin* (on the opposite bank of the Spree around the City Hall and the Molkenmarkt/dairy market), both established in the 13th century. The two areas were connected by the *Mühlendamm*. At the ends of the *Mühlendamm Bridge*, the *fish market* came into being in Cölln and the *dairy market* in Berlin, and near the two markets *St. Peter's Church* (Cölln) and *St. Nicholas' Church* (Berlin). *Littenstrasse* marks the spot of the eastern section of the Berlin city wall.

This district was badly damaged in World War II and has now been rebuilt in modern style. Only a few of the buildings here give us an impression of what old Berlin must have been like. From the *Cathedral* (see p. 55) we follow *Liebknechtstrasse*, which – like the parallel *Rathausstrasse* – has been considerably widened and built up with high-rise apartment houses, stores and the Palace Hotel (luxury class; 13 restaurants) and continue on to the

Marienkirche [58]

St. Mary's Church – after St. Nicholas' Church the second oldest in Berlin – was put up here in the 15th century above the remains of a 13th century structure. The Gothic-like tower received its present form from Langhans in 1790. The *Repentance Cross* outside the church portal is a remembrance of the murder of the provost Nikolaus von Bernau.

Among the sights inside the church are the Baroque *pulpit* by Andreas Schlüter (1703), which was turned to face the choir when the church was restored after the war, and (in the tower hall) the 72-foot long Mediaeval fresco *Dance of Death*, the work of an unknown master, probably created after the plague in 1484. The bronze *baptismal font* in the choir was placed there in 1437. *The church can be visited Mon.–Thurs., 10–12 and 1–5 Sat. 12–4.*

Between Karl-Liebknecht-Strasse and Burgstrasse, behind the Palace Hotel is the *Chapel of the Holy Spirit*, first mentioned as being part of a hospital in 1272. The building adjoining the chapel is in use by the Humboldt University.

St. Mary's Church

The *Fernsehturm* (Television tower) (see p. 60) rises up behind St. Mary's Church. To the south of the church is Begas' *Neptune Fountain,* which once adorned Schlossplatz. The bronze figures on the edges represent what were once four great German rivers – the Rhine, the Elbe, the Oder and the Weichsel.

Rathaus [59]

Old Berlin's City Hall stood on this location as early as the end of the 13th century. The present red brick building (the red bricks are only one of the reasons Berliners call it "Red City Hall") was built between 1861 and 1870 by H.F. Waesemann in Neorenaissance Style. Its 243 foot high, rectangular tower soon became one of Berlin's best known landmarks. There is a frieze running around the building on the level of the second floor, the "Chronicle of Berlin". In 1945 the City Hall was badly damaged (reconstruction in 1955). Two statues remind us of those troubled times: "Reconstruction Helper" and "Woman in the Rubble" by Fritz Cremer on the open area across the way.

Walking southeast from the City Hall, we come to the *Molkenmarkt* (dairy market), the central square of old Berlin, now called *Nikolaikirchplatz,* where we find the restored *Nikolaikirche* (St. Nicholas' Church) [60]. Built around 1230, it is the oldest church in Berlin. It received its three-naved form around 1470. In 1944 it was hit by bombs. Around it, a bit of old Berlin has been resurrected in its Mediaeval garb – the famous "Zum Nussbaum" tavern, the *Ephraim Palace* (fully restored sandstone façade, changing art exhibits, restaurant), the picturesque restaurant "Die Gerichtslaube", as well as many taverns and shops.

The great playwright Gotthold Ephraim Lessing lived at Königsgraben 10 from 1752 to 1766 and completed his famous "Minna von Barnhelm" there. A memorial plaque on Nikolaikirchplatz marks the spot where the house stood till around 1912. At the corner of *Poststrasse* (no. 23) is the classicist *Knoblauch House* (1765; permanent exhibition "Knoblauch Family"), with its "Historische Weinstuben" (Historical Wine House) in the ground floor and on the bank of the Spree the *Reiterstandbild des heiligen Georg* (Equestrian Statue of St. George, 1849).

Walking a little further to the right in the direction of the *Spree*, we see, shortly before the *Mühlendamm Bridge*, on the left in the Mint Building (1935–1939) and in the former Schwerin Palace (built in 1714 with plans by Jean de Bodt) the former *Culture Ministry*. Worked into its façade are Schadow's relief friezes (1798), which formerly adorned the old mint building.

Crossing the *Mühlendamm Bridge*, we come into the *Cöllnischer Fischmarkt* (Cölln fish market) and continue on into *Breite Strasse*, the largest and handsomest road in old Berlin. Only a few of its beautiful houses have been preserved; the *Ermeler House* (1761), for example, was torn down here and put back up on the Märkisches Ufer (today it is a restaurant). No. 35 is the *Ribbeck House* (1624), the only intact Renaissance residential building in Berlin, built as a town house by an aristocratic family made famous here in Fontane's poem ("Sir Ribbeck from Ribbeck in Havel Land"). Attached to this building is the *Alter Marstall* (Old Military Stable; 1665–1670). Inside the *Neuer Marstall* (New Military Stable; 1896–1901) are the city library, the city archives and the city council library.

Two of the houses in nearby *Brüderstrasse*, once a wealthy residential neighborhood, are worth a look: the Nicolaihaus and the "Galgenhaus". The *Nicolai House* (no. 13 – built in 1710) was the home of writer and publisher Friedrich Nicolai from 1787 to 1811. It soon become a meeting place for Berlin's artistic community, frequented by such luminaries as writer Anna Luise Karsch, the artist Chodowiecki, Theodor Körner, Schadow, Schinkel and the composer Carl Friedrich Zelter, who was also a master mason and carried out structural alterations for Nicolai. Memorial plaques remind us of the guests of this house. – The *House of the Gallows* was built around 1680. Tradition has it that an innocent housemaid was hanged here, accused of having stolen a silver spoon from the owner.

The *Jungfernbrücke* (1798) near Brüderstrasse is the last of what were once nine bridges over the Kupfergraben.

Märkisches Museum [60]

Am Köllnischen Park 5, for hours see p. 23. S- and U-Bahn Jannowitzbrücke or U-Bahn Märkisches Museum.

The Mark Brandenburg Museum was founded in 1874 and moved into this mammoth, fortress-like structure in 1908. Its 38 rooms feature exhibitions showing the historical development of the city of Berlin from its beginnings to the present day. One striking display is religious art from the pre-Reformation period.

On the ground floor we can look at finds from Berlin's prehistory and the early history of the city, as well as some very interesting models showing the city around 1440 and 1750, and items which go back to the dawn of the industrial era.

On the second floor we can get an overview of *Berlin's Theatre History* from 1740 to the present. Here we also find *Berlin glasswork, faiences* and *porcelain.* The third floor has exhibitions of *Berlin painting* and *applied arts,* as well as a *collection of mechanical musical instruments* from the Baroque era to the present. Further collections belonging to the museum may be seen at St. Nicholas' Church, Ephraim Palace, Knoblauch House, the Handwerksmuseum (Handicrafts Museum, Mühlendamm 5) and the Museum Berliner Arbeiterleben (Museum of Working-Class Berlin, Husemannstrasse 12). Behind the museum is the small *Köllnischer Park*, containing a remnant of the former city wall, a little tower (1658), an enclosure where bears are kept and a *Zille Monument* by H. Drake.

At Märkisches Ufer 16–18, in two old Berlin residential buildings (17th and 18th centuries), the *Otto Nagel House* has been established. It shows paintings, pastels and drawings by this Berlin artist. There is an apartment building from the end of the 18th century at Märkisches Ufer 14. No. 12 is a copy of a Rococo house from the Friedrichsgracht. No. 10 is the *Ermeler House,* transplanted here from Breite Strasse and Berlin's last Rococo house.

From the Märkisches Museum, you can take the U-Bahn to *Alexanderplatz* and continue on from there to *Karl-Marx-Allee*. If you're up for a walk, then let us recommend a little detour: cross the *Spree* over the *Jannowitz Bridge*. Then, shortly afterward, turn left into the *Rolandufer*, then diagonally to your right into *Waisenstrasse*. Here, at the site of Berlin's Mediaeval city limits, remnants of the *city wall* (dating from the 13th and 14th centuries) were found (on the right side of the street). A little farther away, on the right, you will find a historical tavern called "Zur letzten Instanz" (Final Appeal; 16th century), and on the left-hand side, in *Parochialstrasse,* the large *Parochial Church* (1695–1703), which was badly damaged in the war and has thus far only been provided with the most urgent renovations. We now turn into *Klosterstrasse.* Here we find the remains of the *Klosterkirche* (Cloister Church; 14th century), which was once part of the Franciscan monastery of the "Grey Brothers", where the Mark Brandenburg's oldest secondary school was housed, the "Berlin Academy in the Grey Monastery". Its most renowned alumnus was Bismarck. *Grunerstrasse* then leads on to:

Alexanderplatz

A brand new city center has grown up recently around Alexanderplatz, known here simply as "Alex". The 1,200 foot high *Fernsehturm* (Television Tower) the Berliners call the "Telesparagus" was completed in 1969 and today dominates the city. There is an observation area with a magnificent view in the steel ball at the 666 foot level and above it the "Tele-Café" turns once around its axis every hour. In 1964 the *House of the Teacher,* with a monumental frieze, and beside it the *Kongresshalle* (Congress Hall) were built on the east side of the square. The "Berolina Skyscraper" is one of the older buildings still intact here, as is the "Alexanderhaus". Newly added buildings include the new "Centrum Department Store", the 39-story Hotel "Stadt Berlin" (casino), the pedestrian tunnel, the international clock and the "Fountain of Friendship of the Peoples".

Karl-Marx-Allee

Karl-Marx-Allee (until 1961 named Stalinallee) combines with its extension, *Frankfurter Allee,* to run some three miles to the east. It is one of East Berlin's showpiece boulevards. Six to nine storey buildings, their style reminiscent of Soviet institutional architecture, line the street. From *Strausberger Platz, Lichtenberger Strasse* leads on to *Leninplatz* with *Lenin Monument* (dating from 1970).

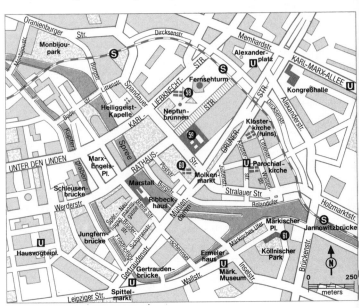

To get to Köpenick and Erkner, it's best to take the S-Bahn line that goes from Wannsee via the Zoo, Alexanderplatz and Ostkreuz to Erkner.

Köpenick,

which is by far the largest district in all of Berlin, is also the district richest in lakes and forests (Müggelsee, Langer See, Seddinsee, Zeuthener See, Große Krampe).

The heart of Köpenick is the old part of the city found on the island formed by the Spree and Dahme. It can be reached by going from the S-Bahn station in Köpenick via Bahnhofstrasse.

Not far from the Laurentiuskirche (St. Lawrence Church; 1841) with its high red brick gabled roof is the City Hall, a neo-Gothic red brick building (1904) which has earned dubious renown some 85 years ago.

The whole world laughed about the bogus "Hauptmann von Köpenick" ("Captain of Köpenick"), the shoemaker Wilhelm Voigt, who disguised himself as a Prussian officer and arrested the mayor of Köpenick on October 16, 1906. Wilhelm Voigt then disappeared with the town treasury.

The German writer Carl Zuckmayer used this incident as the basis for his play of the same name.

In Kietz, between Gartenstrasse and Kietzstrasse, fisher cottages dating from 17th and 18th centuries still stand. They remind us that Köpenick was founded as a fishing village many centuries ago – in 1209.

The baroque castle, located not far from the City Hall on the castle island, has housed the Museum of Applied Arts since 1963. European arts and crafts from the late Middle Ages to the present can be found there.

The collection of furniture is quite extensive.

Furthermore, you should take special note of Empress Gisela's jewelry (10th–11th century) and the Berlin silver buffet of the Prussian King Frederick I (1695–1698). In the near future this collection will be merged with the one in the Museum of Applied Arts in the Tiergarten.

The castle was built from 1677–1683 by the Dutch Rutger von Langerfeldt on the grounds of one of Elector Joachim II's hunting lodges.

Each year the "Köpenick Summer", a popular folk festival, takes place in the castle gardens.

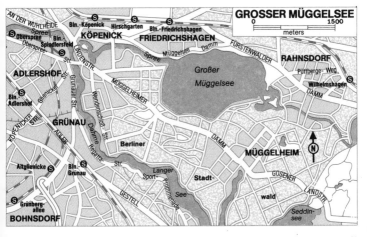

Other Sights to See in the Eastern Section

*Museum für Naturkunde

Invalidenstrasse 43. Hours: see p. 23.

The Natural History Museum was put up in 1889 and contains three museums: the *Zoological,* the *Geological* and the *Mineralogical Museum.* Special attractions of the public museums include *skeletons of giant dinosaurs* and the *imprint of the archaeopteryx,* a prehistoric bird.

Prenzlauer Berg

This lower middle-class district, which borders on the city district Mitte, has developed its own subculture just as western Kreuzberg has. 40 % of all apartments facing back courtyards in the eastern section of the city are found here. Some streets were restored in connection with celebration of Berlin's 750th anniversary, e.g. the old Berlin Husemannstrasse, where you find, among other things, a hairdressers' museum. Sophienstrasse, which borders Alexanderplatz and is in the northern part of what was once the "Scheunenviertel" ("barn quarter"), has been restored, but many courtyards and old Berlin buildings, such as the former School for the Blind in Gipsstrasse 11, are in a state of disrepair. – Prenzlauer Allee 80 is the address of the Zeiss-Grossplanetarium (open Tues.–Fri. 1–8, Sat. and Sun. 9:30–5).

Sowjetisches Ehrenmal

The Soviet Memorial is located in the 195 acre *Treptow Park,* laid out in 1885. Behind the main entrance is a grey marble statue of "Mother Homeland", then two huge red marble pylons representing lowered flags. The actual field of honor is the final resting place for 4,800 of the 20,000 Soviet soldiers who died in the battle of Berlin. The memorial ends at a *Hill of Honor,* in which an additional 200 Soviet soldiers are buried, with a 108 foot *mausoleum* crowned by a 42-foot high bronze statue of a Red Army soldier carrying a rescued child in his arms, his sword lowered on a broken swastika.

Synagogue

The Synagogue on Oranienburger Strasse 30 was built between 1859–1866 and then destroyed on Crystal Night (Nov. 9, 1938) by Nazi thugs, who left only the facade intact. The building is now being restored in its original Moorish style and it will serve as the "New Synagogue-Centrum Judaicum".

*Tierpark Berlin in Friedrichsfelde

Open in summer from 7, in winter from 8 until sundown, admission charge.

This 395 acre zoological garden (the zoo in West Berlin has a mere 82 acres) was opened in 1955. Most of the approximately 7,500 animals (almost 900 species, including deer, elephants, kangaroos bisons, pelicans) live in open enclosures. One special attraction is the *Alfred Brehm House* with lion and tiger rocks, tropical building, pachyderm and crocodile houses and penguin and gibbon enclosures. *Schloss Friedrichsfelde* (1690–1719) with its historical apartments has been restored.

Volkspark Friedrichshain

This park, the city's oldest (1848), starts at *Leninplatz* to the north of *Strausberger Platz.* The 131 acre facility contains an open-air theatre, two rubble mountains, and a "Fairy Tale Fountain".

Cemeteries

Dorotheenstadt and Friedrichswerder Cemeteries (on *Chausseestrasse*), Berlin's most important historical cemetery: here lie the philosophers *Fichte* (1762–1814) and *Hegel* (1770–1831), the architect *Schinkel* (1781–1841), the playwright *Bertolt Brecht* (1898–1956) and the novelist *Heinrich Mann* (1871–1950).

In the *French Cemetery (Chausseestrasse 127)* we find the grave of copperplate engraver *Chodowiecki* (1726–1832).

The *Invalid Cemetery (Scharnhorststrasse)* contains the graves of *Scharnhorst* (1755–1813), *von Schlieffen* (1833–1913) and *von Seeckt* (1866–1936).

In the *Sophia Cemetery (Grosse Hamburger Strasse)* you will find the graves of composer *Karl-Friedrich Zelter* and historian *Leopold von Ranke.*

The *Jewish Cemetery* in Weissensee *(Herbert-Baum-Strasse)* is one of the largest Jewish cemeteries in Europe and contains the graves of *Lesser Ury, Samuel Fischer* and *Theodor Wolff.* It was ceremoniously reopened in 1986.

The *Old Jewish Cemetery (Schönhauser Allee 25)* contains the graves of the composer *Giacomo Meyerbeer* (1791–1864) and the painter *Max Liebermann* (1847–1935).

Potsdam

Potsdam (population: 143,000), the "most beautiful suburb of Berlin" *(Jean Paul)*, since 1990 the capital of the new State of Brandenburg, is located in the midst of the peaceful forest and lake countryside along the Havel River in southwest Berlin. Potsdam, whose documented history goes back to 933 when it was first mentioned as the Slavic fishermen's village Poztupimi, will celebrate its 1000th anniversary in 1993. You can best reach the city via the Glienicke Bridge.

The Prussian kings, who built their castles here, gave Potsdam its distinctive appearance. The most important artists of their day contributed to the design of castle and gardens, regarded as one of the prime achievements of the 18th and early 19th centuries: artists working here under Frederick the Great included, in addition to Knobelsdorff, Büring, Manger and Gontard, under Frederick William III and Frederick William IV Schinkel, Persius and Stüler and the landscape gardener Lenné. The actual city has a modern downtown area, with restorations of the *Old City Hall*, the *Knobelsdorff House* and *St. Nicholas' Church*. The royal town house and the garrison church have been torn down.

Other sights worth seeing are the traditional *Dutch Quarter*, with its brick buildings from the mid-18th century, which are, however, in desparate need of repair, and the Russian settlement *Alexandrowka* (1826). Its log cabins are built in Russian style, but they, too, are in a state of disrepair.

**Schloss Sanssouci

Sans Souci Palace was built in Rococo style by G.W. von Knobelsdorff between 1745 and 1747, based on Frederick the Great's ideas. One particularly impressive point is the 318 foot long front facade with its protuberant, domed central structure.

The *interior is decorated in magnificent Rococo and contains a wealth of art treasures and reminiscences of *Frederick II.* Of prime interest here are the *library,* the *small gallery* and the *music room.* Here in Sans Souci, his favorite residence, Frederick the Great died on August 17, 1786.

The east section of the magnificent *Castle Garden* was laid out by Knobelsdorff in the form of French parterre gardens. The western section was created by Büring and Manger in Anglo-Chinese style at the time of construction of the *New Palace,* based on a design by Frederick the Great.

Also worth seeing in Sans Souci park are the *Chinese Tea House* (1754–1756), Schinkel's *Roman Baths* (1850), based on an ancient Roman villa, and the *Orangerie* with its *Raphael Hall* (copies), built in 1850 by Persius and Stüler in Florentine style. The little *Charlottenhof Castle* was designed by Schinkel in 1826 for Crown Prince Frederick William. After over 40 years, Frederick III's *Mausoleum* has now been reopened to the public.

Cecilienhof Castle in the *New Garden,* built as an English-style hunting lodge from 1913 to 1917, was where the Potsdam Agreement of 1945 was signed.

Sans Souci Palace with terraced vineyards

63

Index